James Keith Trotter

**The Niger Sources and the Borders of the new Sierra Leone Protectorate**

James Keith Trotter

**The Niger Sources and the Borders of the new Sierra Leone Protectorate**

ISBN/EAN: 9783743317352

Manufactured in Europe, USA, Canada, Australia, Japa

Cover: Foto ©ninafisch / pixelio.de

Manufactured and distributed by brebook publishing software (www.brebook.com)

James Keith Trotter

**The Niger Sources and the Borders of the new Sierra Leone Protectorate**

# THE NIGER SOURCES

## AND THE BORDERS OF THE NEW SIERRA LEONE PROTECTORATE

BY
LIEUT.-COL. J. K. TROTTER, R.A.

WITH FOUR FULL-PAGE ILLUSTRATIONS AND A MAP

METHUEN & CO.
36 ESSEX STREET, W.C.
LONDON
1898

# CONTENTS

### CHAPTER I
FROM LIVERPOOL TO FREETOWN - - - - - 1

### CHAPTER II
THE JOURNEY TO THE NIGER SOURCES - - - 19

### CHAPTER III
THE WESTERN WATERSHED OF THE NIGER - - 60

### CHAPTER IV
THROUGH SALIMA AND KAMUKE COUNTRY TO THE KABA RIVER - - - - - - - - 95

### CHAPTER V
FROM THE LITTLE TO THE GREAT SKARSIES - - 124

### CHAPTER VI
RETURN TO THE COAST AND EMBARKATION FOR ENGLAND - - - - - - - - - 146

### CHAPTER VII
THE PEOPLE OF THE SIERRA LEONE PROTECTORATE 163

### CHAPTER VIII
THE DEVELOPMENT OF THE INTERIOR, AND THE INFLUENCE UPON IT OF THE HEALTH QUESTION 183

### CHAPTER IX
THE GEOGRAPHY AND TOPOGRAPHY OF THE SIERRA LEONE PROTECTORATE - - - - - - 205

APPENDIX - - - - - - - - - 228

# LIST OF ILLUSTRATIONS

                                                                     PAGE

THE NIGER NEAR ITS SOURCE - - - *Frontispiece*

KURANKO BOWMAN - - - - - - - 42

THE KING OF TAMISSO AND HIS SUITE - - - 131

DANCE OF A BUNDI PRIEST ON OCCASION OF CEREMONY 182

MAP - - - - - - - - - - 238

## NOTE

THE FOUR ILLUSTRATIONS IN THIS BOOK ARE FROM PHOTOGRAPHS BY CAPTAIN PASSAGA, THE PRESIDENT OF THE FRENCH DELIMITING COMMISSION.

# CHAPTER I

## FROM LIVERPOOL TO FREETOWN

THE expedition described in this work was undertaken with the object of marking out on the ground the boundary between French Guinea and Sierra Leone, which had been agreed upon between Great Britain and France on January 21st, 1895. The protocol signed that day was the outcome of negotiations which had lasted for many years, and until the boundary question was settled, nothing could be done towards developing the interior of the country. Of the ground covered by the agreement absolutely nothing was known except at one or two points; and it will be remembered that in 1894 a British and French force had come accidentally into collision at Waima, owing partly to the unsettled state of the country and partly to the general uncertainty concerning the frontiers. The region of the Niger sources was visited by Laing in the early part of the century, and the actual source by Zweifel and Moustier in 1879, but in the works of these travellers few topographical details are given, nor is it possible to locate the position with reference to any known point in the interior. French officers have also passed through the country at the head of the Niger in recent years, but they have left no public record of their journeys. It was, therefore, necessary that the boundary as agreed upon should be marked out and sketched by a joint Commission, and I was appointed to act for the British Government in this matter, being assisted by Lieutenant (local Captain) Tyler, R.E., who was at the time stationed at Sierra Leone.

The journey to Freetown occupies from thirteen to sixteen days. Probably not many people realize that, with the exception of the imperial ports of Gibraltar and Malta, the Gambia and Sierra Leone are the nearest

British possessions to the mother country. As regards time, it is true, these settlements are farther from our shores than British North America, for hitherto English people have discovered few good reasons for visiting West Africa, and some very cogent ones for keeping away from it. Liverpool alone has undertaken the conquest of the land, and through Liverpool all the trade between Great Britain and this part of Africa passes. The passenger traffic is so limited that the boats of the African Steamship Company and the British and African Line, which run in conjunction with each other, are easily able to deal with it. These boats rarely exceed 3000 tons gross, and their highest speed under favourable circumstances is not more than 10 knots.

The direct boats call at Grand Canary, and the intermediate ones at Madeira, Teneriffe, and Dakar. It seems a special provision of Providence that the Canary Group and Madeira, probably the finest health resorts in the world, lie so close to the deadly West African coast, and are so easily accessible to invalids from

Gambia, Sierra Leone, the Gold Coast, Lagos, and the Niger. These islands are well worth a visit. Madeira is well known to health seekers, but of late years its monopoly in the North Atlantic has been seriously threatened by the Canary Group. At Grand Canary the Spanish authorities are constructing a breakwater, and in a few years' time they will be able to offer to ocean steamers a secure harbour. The fruit trade has been largely developed through the enterprise of Messrs. Elder, Dempster & Co., the agents of the African Steamship Co., and a large number of visitors from the United Kingdom, as well as from the West Coast, spend the winter and spring in the island, the climate of which is drier than that of Madeira.

From Grand Canary to Sierra Leone the West African steamers take about six days. As one approaches the coast the air becomes humid and heavy, and the change from the drier climate of the north-east trades is a little depressing. Passing up the broad estuary of the Sierra Leone river, the boats hug the southern shore, and afford an excellent view of the towns and country which make up the little colony of Sierra Leone. Whatever may be said against the country from other points of view, the severest critic cannot find a word to say against its beauty as viewed from the deck of a steamer. Freetown, with its outlying villages, nestling amongst vegetation rich, varied, and luxuriant, backed by the forest-clad Lion mountains and faced by the distant low, palm-fringed Bullom shore, makes a charming picture, one difficult to reproduce, but not easy to forget. The place does not improve on closer acquaintance. The town is poorly built, and not worthy of the position a place of its importance should occupy. The only respectable buildings are Government House on Tower Hill, and just above it the barracks of half a battalion of the West India regiment, to which is attached a very good swimming bath. The height of this position is 300 feet above the sea. At a height of 800 feet are some new barracks on Mount Auriol for the other half battalion, and still higher up, 1500 feet above sea level, is a sanatorium. Fruit, vegetables, and fish are plentiful in the town, but of cows in a public capacity nothing is known, and I could hear of but one horse in the place. The milkman to the colony is Switzerland, and the butterman Denmark.

Whether it is due to want of enterprise that horses and cows are not to be found about Freetown, or whether it is the case, as I have heard stated, that they cannot exist in the place, I am not in a position to decide. It cannot, however, be due to want of forage, for both grain and herbage are abundant, and if it is due to climate, the conditions peculiar to Freetown must be limited to the actual coast line, for cows are to be met with a very few miles inland in country which, as regards climate, belongs to the coast region.

In and about Freetown no roads exist in the meaning of the word as understood in Europe. The streets are broad, but they are merely unlevel green expanses, with foot-tracks running across them. Road ballasting, road drainage, and road levelling are expressions unknown in a land where the wheel has not yet been introduced in any form.

The shops of Freetown are less imposing than those of European capitals, though they follow the modern practice in that the small tradesman is swamped by the big trading company. They apparently do not seek to entice the passer-by by a meretricious display of their most captivating wares, and an advertisement of their cheapest prices; but the would-be purchaser enters unsolicited a large galvanized iron barn, where the obliging counterman hands him anything he asks for, from a pair of trousers to a tomahawk, whilst around him crowds of natives, in every costume and of every colour, are chattering, bargaining, and laughing over their purchases. Singularly enough the leading shop of Freetown is that of a French Company (*Compagnie Française de l'Afrique Occidentale*), which has trading stations all along the West Coast, and which is much patronized by British residents in Sierra Leone. This establishment has been carried on with success whilst many British companies have failed to do sufficient paying business, and have disappeared one after another. There are, however, still one or two British companies in the place which combine trading with other business, and being backed by men of large capital and influence, continue to make their way.

The buildings in the town of Freetown are one and all bad, not only from the artistic but even more from the sanitary point of view, and they are singularly destitute of anything which can contribute to comfort or convenience. The town is very badly lighted with oil lamps, which at best do no more than illuminate the lamp post which supports them, and a stranger visiting the town on a dark night may consider himself fortunate if he does not explore the bottom of many pitfalls. But the town is now a municipality, and it may be hoped that in a few years' time it will see many improvements inaugurated.

What specially strikes the casual visitor to Freetown is the complete absence of any form of organized amusement or recreation amongst the British residents, and of any common meeting ground for the promotion of social intercourse. This may be due to the enervating effect of the climate, but one cannot help speculating on the good which might be done by anything which would promote activity and raise the spirits. Lawn tennis is played a little by a few of the more energetic, a little shooting is attempted, and a little boating. "At homes," etc., are given at Government House, and occasionally the band of the West India regiment plays, but beyond this I heard of nothing in the way of recreation.

The climate of Sierra Leone has an evil reputation, which is too deeply engraved on the headstones of Kissi Cemetery to be open to any qualification. Nevertheless I believe it has seen its worst days, and if only the assistance of modern science is called in, it may yet become a moderately healthy place. It possesses the enormous advantage of a pure water supply, probably the only thoroughly sound water on the West Coast. If this water was laid on to the whole of the town, if the population, both European and native, could be induced to use it with the least possible adulteration, and if, finally, a comprehensive scheme of drainage were carried out, a marked improvement in health would certainly result. The position of Freetown is one of so great importance as to justify the adoption of every modern means of promoting the health of both Europeans and natives. As the only good harbour in West Africa, the terminus of the railway line to the interior now being constructed, and the only imperial coaling station in the North Atlantic, it has a great future before it. It is on the direct line to the Cape, and is most conveniently situated as a coaling station, being about eight days' steaming, at 13 knots, from Southampton, and very much the same distance from Cape Town. Yet, in spite of the advantages of its position, vessels are sent two or three hundred miles out of their course to coal at St. Vincent in the Cape Verde Islands, anchoring in an exposed roadstead, off a barren coast, where the coaling arrangements are of the worst, and where no fresh provisions are to be had. A little enterprise on the part of the Sierra Leone people should make their harbour the port of call for vessels bound both to South Africa and to the Pacific, as well as for those homeward bound from those parts.

The history of Sierra Leone is too well known to need repetition here, but there are probably many in England ignorant that the small colony proper is inhabited by a population whose only language is English, if indeed a language can be called English, which, as spoken by the lower classes, no dweller in our islands could interpret. I speak only of the Sierra Leonis, the inhabitants of Freetown and the neighbouring villages, the descendants of freed slaves. In addition to these there is a large floating population of natives from the interior, trading or seeking work, who speak different languages and dialects. The Sierra Leonis themselves, however, so far as I could learn, have no knowledge of the interior or sympathy with questions affecting a frontier policy, and it appears to be unfortunate that the Protectorate which has recently been established over the native tribes of the interior should bear the name of Sierra Leone, which must ever be associated with a peculiar and most interesting chapter in the history of Africa.

Amongst the Sierra Leone people are many highly educated gentlemen, employed as lawyers, doctors, merchants, clergymen, government officials, and in other capacities, a great part of whom have been educated in England, and are quite able to hold their own with any Europeans. I have stated that the Sierra Leone people are not interested in questions of the interior, but one conspicuous exception should be mentioned in the person of Mr. Parkes, the Superintendent of Native Affairs, a gentleman of the highest attainments, educated at Oxford, who has a thorough knowledge of all matters connected with the interior, and who is in constant communication with the Chiefs in the Protectorate. Mr. Parkes has accompanied the Governor on his expeditions throughout the country, and his knowledge of all frontier questions is second only to that of His Excellency. Our expedition, as regards transport and supply, was organized entirely by him. The food for the Europeans had to be carried with us, as nothing except rice, and occasionally fowls and sheep, and possibly now and again a bullock, could be obtained up country, and arrangements had to be made for collecting rice for the natives at various points. We had, moreover, to carry tents, instruments, ammunition, and hammocks, so that a large number of carriers was required, and depots had to be formed at Falaba and at Sangbaia near Kurubundo. A large force of carriers was engaged, and the men were mustered in gangs of from twenty to thirty, each under a head-man. We had also from six to eight men to each hammock, servants, two interpreters, and ten Frontier Police, our entire force numbering, to commence with—in addition to the two Commissioners, Captain M'Kee of the Frontier Police, and Dr. Paris, a colonial surgeon—4 sappers R.E., and 448 natives.

Some twelve days after our arrival at Sierra Leone the French Commissioners landed at Freetown, and about the same time the Governor, Colonel Cardew, returned from England. A meeting was speedily arranged to discuss the method of procedure, and it was thereat agreed that the two Commissioners should proceed at once to the Niger sources, there to begin their boundary demarcation. The boundary in Samu from the Atlantic coast to the Mola river, an affluent of the Great Skarsies, was to be demarcated by the junior French Commissioners, of whom there were three, the British being represented by an officer to be selected by the Governor.

The President of the French Commission, Captain Passaga of the Marine Infantry, is an officer of great reputation as a topographer, and has served in the topographical section of the French War Office, and on the survey of Algeria. He also took part in the Dahome campaign. The second officer, Captain Cayrade, of the Marine Artillery, was specially selected for astronomical work. He had served in the French Sudan, and had been stationed at Heremakono, close to the Anglo-French frontier. The third officer, Captain Millot, had seen much service in the Sudan, and had taken part in several of the campaigns against the Sofas. His knowledge of the country and the natives specially fitted him for the work of delimiting the frontier.

On December 16th the joint Commission embarked in the Governor's yacht, the "Countess of Derby," the native followers being towed astern in lighters. The French party consisted of the two senior Commissioners, one European under officer, ten Senegalese soldiers, ninety-two carriers and servants, with four riding mules. Having no hammocks, and having arranged a service of supplies from their Sudan stations, they were able to do with a much smaller establishment than we required. The third Commissioner, Captain Millot, with one European under officer, proceeded from Konakri, the capital of French Guinea, to the Niger sources, and joined the Commission there some days after we had reached Tembi Kunda, the first projected arrangement for delimiting the Samu frontier having fallen through. We steamed up the Sierra Leone river to the Port Lokko creek, and on the morning of the 17th reached Moferri, the highest point navigable by the steam yacht. Here we cast off the lighters, transferred ourselves into the "Countess of Derby's" boats, and, after rowing hard for some hours, reached Port Lokko, a large native town on a tidal creek, where we disembarked and arranged our loads.

Port Lokko is a town situated in Timmeni country, and is part of the colony of Sierra Leone. It contains a police barrack, a mission station, a store, and a grog shop, the only one we met with in British territory till our return to Freetown. We were lodged in the best house available in the place, a somewhat pretentious building, containing several rooms and one or two pieces of European furniture.

We had now reached the limits of British territory as represented by the colony of Sierra Leone. The country beyond this was at the time we passed through it merely what is known in diplomatic parlance as a British 'sphere of influence,' or, in other words, native territory under native laws and jurisdiction, which was recognized by the neighbouring European powers as bound by treaty to Great Britain. The Chiefs of this country, so far as it had been explored, received occasional messages from the Governor of Sierra Leone, and exchanged greetings with him, and some of them, whose people occupied country through which trade routes passed, received small annual subsidies for keeping the roads open.

The colony of Sierra Leone is limited to the peninsula of Sierra Leone, to British Kwaia, to Sherboro, and the country within immediate reach of the coast line and the navigable embouchures of the rivers. There is, I believe, no very definite boundary on the land side, but actual jurisdiction does not extend farther inland than the immediate neighbourhood of British posts and factories.

We had the usual palaver with the Chief of Port Lokko, who is also Chief of a district of Timmeni country bearing the same name. At night a tom-tom procession was organized by the natives, who kept up a great uproar till early morning, to which a good day's work happily rendered us insensible.

## CHAPTER II

## THE JOURNEY TO THE NIGER SOURCES

OUR instructions were to march *viâ* Bumban to Kruto, and from thence to find a route to Kurubundo and onwards to Tembi Kunda, the head of the Tembi river, which is the longest affluent of the Niger. Having reached this point we were to fix a line running due westward from it to the watershed between the Niger and the rivers running westwards, and we were then to follow the watershed, which forms the boundary, in a northerly direction, till it cut the tenth parallel of north latitude, where the first section of the boundary delimitation was to end.

As regards the march up country, the first stage was from Port Lokko to Bumban. Throughout this section we followed a well-known trade route, and it was therefore unnecessary for us to survey it, but, in order to check the position of our halting places, we took daily observations for latitude, and we used a perambulator to give the distances accomplished on each march.

We left Port Lokko on December 18th, and covering a distance, according to the perambulator, of $77\frac{1}{2}$ miles, reached Bumban on the 24th. The road, which resembles all West African main lines of communication, is a narrow winding track, not unlike a footpath through a wood in England in summer time. Swamps, creeks, and streams are frequently crossed, and the country, without being so densely covered with bush as the valleys further inland, is yet so close and so flat that nothing can be seen in any direction. The winding path is invisible 20 or 30 yards ahead, and though one has constantly the impression that the next few yards will bring one to a point from which a view can be obtained, this point is never reached. We passed through this country in as complete ignorance of what lay to our right and left as if we had been blindfolded; the very villages we entered were not recognizable till the banana leaves, the unmistakable indication of native habitations, were almost within reach. It is curious to notice the influence of their surroundings on the peoples of the interior. There the natives live in single file. If you watch them as they pass over the open spaces occupied by villages or cultivation, you will never see them in any other formation, and if you endeavour, as we did, to form them in line to beat patches of ground for game, in two or three minutes at most you will find them serpentining across country one behind another. The roads are originally made winding in order to avoid the numerous obstacles which cannot be cleared away, but whether from the crooked nature of the tracks or from some other cause, no native appears to be able to walk straight. A caravan passing through the bush moves as if it were following the trail of a serpent, and on the one or two occasions when we crossed perfectly open ground, the direction followed was precisely the same; instead of taking a bee line from point to point, the long column executed a series of windings and curves. There is, perhaps, another explanation of the inability of the natives to walk in a straight line, besides the curved nature of the roads, though it is connected with the same cause, and this is that, as shoes are not worn, the feet are very sensitive to anything likely to cut or bruise them, and therefore the natives acquire a habit of picking their way to avoid obstacles, and of regularly deviating to right and left of the general direction they are following.

During this march we crossed, near Madina, the Mabole river, an affluent of the Little Skarsies or Kaba. It is here a large river, some 90 yards in width, and unfordable at any season. We passed our loads across in two dug-out canoes of poor construction and very little buoyancy. During the operation one of the canoes foundered and sank. It was recovered, and the water was being baled out with a large calabash, when I heard piercing screams from the branches of a tree behind me. The Chief of Madina was watching the crossing from this elevated position, and I learned from the interpreter that the calabash used for baling was his property, and that the effect of dipping it in what he termed "crocodile water" would be that he would be eaten by a crocodile. We endeavoured to console him by pointing out the satisfaction he ought to feel when the contingency arose at being eaten in such a good cause, but his mind evidently dwelt mainly on the personal discomfort of the process, and it was only by taking the law into our own hands that we could continue to use the royal vessel.

The only other river crossed during this stage was the Belia, an affluent of the Mabole, which we passed near Rotata, and which in the dry season is fordable. This river separates the Safroko Timmeni from the Sanda Lokko country, the Mabole at Madina being the division between Sanda Lokko and Biriwa Limba country.

The climate during this march was in all

respects that of the coast region. The air was heavy and somewhat depressing, and the difference between day and night temperature was small. In this country a very little exertion produces a great deal of moisture, and a few miles of marching effected a saturation of one's wearing apparel which was a little uncomfortable. This is no doubt due to the air being charged with moisture, a condition which made the temperature very much less supportable than that accompanying a dry heat. We did not use a maximum and minimum thermometer, but registering the temperature in the early morning, and again after reaching our halting-place, *i.e.* between 10 A.M. and noon, we found the lowest temperature noted to be 70°, and the mean of the early morning readings to be 72.5°. The highest reading was 84°, and the lowest of the day readings 81°. Exertion at this stage was not an unmixed delight.

After crossing the Mabole, as we approached Bumban, we became aware of a change in our surroundings. Hills were visible ahead of us, and the road we followed led us past huge boulders of granite. We found Bumban to be a large town lying on low ground, some 300 feet above sea level, and shut in by hills on all sides but the west. It contains a police barracks, occupied by a detachment of Frontier Police, and is the seat of the Chief of the Biriwa Limba, a man who appears to be held in the greatest dread by his subjects, although he rules them without the assistance of any executive. Even our own followers had a superstitious dread of his power to hurt them so long as we continued in his country, which was of some value as a means of preventing marauding.

Captain Tyler, our photographer, endeavoured to obtain a photograph of the Chief's wives, but unfortunately his plates were not large enough to include the whole establishment, which is said to number 300, so he had to be content with a small selection. The photograph, however, failed; but he succeeded in developing one of the Chief feeding his pigeons, which are even more numerous than his wives, and which he treats with more devotion so far as we observed.

We halted at Bumban on Christmas day, and entertained our French comrades. A halt indeed involved as much labour as a day's march, with the observations to be taken, calculations to be worked out, despatches for the mail to be prepared, and other work to be undertaken. There was, in addition to the routine tasks, the discipline and administration of our native establishment to be seen to, and their commissariat requirements to be provided for. Even now these matters pressed upon us, and as we advanced further into the interior they became a source of daily anxiety.

A part of our daily work, both on marching and on halting days, was the palaver with the Chief of the place and his people. These interviews differed from each other only in the varying degree of importance attached to the occasion, the Chief on some occasions being the paramount ruler of a country or district, in others merely the head-man of a town or village. But in all cases the procedure was the same, and the following description, which applies in the first instance to our palaver with the Chief of Biriwa Limba, will serve as an example of the way these meetings are conducted in West Africa.

An hour would be agreed upon, and the Chief would send round to every part of his dominions within reach and collect his people by beat of tom-tom. At the given time they would assemble, generally in some open space near the town, under a cotton tree or round a conspicuous object—occasionally the people assembled in front of the hut which we occupied, but the important palavers were more frequently held outside the town. A semicircle would be formed, the Chief and his most important followers being in front. Opposite to them we took our places, our chairs having been previously placed for us. Beside us stood our escort of Frontier Police, and the clerk attached to the Commission, an official from the department of Native Affairs. The Chief then made a long address, which, as translated by the interpreter into Sierra Leone English, and with the assistance of our doctor rendered into English as comprehended by us, was boiled down through a few meaningless platitudes into the information that he was very glad to see us, repeated many times, and into the prayer that we would accept the present prepared for us, which was laid out before us. This consisted in general of some bowls of rice, perhaps a few kola nuts, which are of considerable value in this country, and are the emblem of friendship and welcome, with the addition, according to the wealth of the Chief, of a couple of fowls, a sheep, or perhaps a bullock. Whilst this performance was going on, the clerk, who was a past master in the etiquette of these proceedings, made a hurried estimate of the value of the Chief's present and disappeared. The proper course, I believe, is that the receiver of the present, *i.e.* the visitor, should always, to use a vulgarism, go one better, but I am not sure that this principle is rigidly adhered to in parts of the country where the value of trade goods is little understood. To pay for presents received we had with us a large stock of wares, many being of no value except at places near the coast. The principal articles of trade were Manchester cottons, fancy smoking caps, penny looking-glasses, tobacco leaves, Florida water, much appreciated by the natives when mixed with tobacco; hair-oil, used to anoint the face; salt, beads, threepenny pieces for making necklaces, and other small things of a portable nature. Whilst our return present was being prepared, I replied to the Chief's address. I was not master of the elocution (and circumlocution) he employed, but I merely said I was glad to see him, I thanked him for his present, and I begged his acceptance of ours. I explained also the business we were engaged upon. Many of the Chiefs would hardly believe that we were not, to use the expressive phrase of the country, bringing a war with us. In the boundary districts I always explained the run of the frontier, and dwelt on the enormity of interfering with the landmarks we had set up. I also impressed on the Chief that he was to "clean" or "brush" his roads, as it is expressed, and to increase his farm lands. By the time these words had passed through the interpreter, our present had arrived, and it was interesting, especially in the remoter parts of the country, to observe the childish delight with which the natives examined the cottons, the looking-glasses, and the tobacco. Men who had probably never before had an opportunity of studying their own personal attractions gazed solemnly for many minutes on their features as reflected by a very inferior glass. Tobacco is grown everywhere, but it is of poor quality, and the trade article is greatly appreciated. It is mixed with Florida water, when this luxury is obtainable, and made into snuff, which is carried in a small cylindrical box, and administered to the expectant nostril, by those of high rank, with an ivory spoon. Cottons are also highly valued. Cotton is grown everywhere, and the native women card and weave it, producing a strong cloth, which is generally dyed by being dipped in the juice of the leaves of the indigo plant; but the process is very slow and costly, and I imagine that for any one but the Chief to get a new suit of clothes is a rare event.

# THE JOURNEY

Occasionally, especially in Kuranko country, music was introduced on these occasions, the instrument in common use being composed of a series of strips of wood of graduated length, fastened over gourds. The performer, who wears iron bracelets to add to the sound, plays this instrument with a stick shod with rubber. The music consists of a chant of half a dozen chords, repeated *ad lib.*, and accompanying a vocal performance of a monotonous description.

As soon as the palaver was over we were able to bargain with the Chief for rice or fowls, or whatever we required, but etiquette forbids that any negotiations of a commercial nature should be entered into until the presents have been exchanged.

From Bumban our next objective was Kruto (or Kru) in Kuranko country. This town lay, so far as we knew, nearly due east of Bumban, but the intervening country was densely covered with bush and untracked. Every inquiry was made, but we were informed that no direct roads existed. The only known route was that of the Falaba road to Lenge-

koro, and thence to Koinadugu. This involved an enormous circuit, and, as time was of the greatest importance to us, I endeavoured to find some way of shortening the distance. We started on 26th December along the Falaba road, and as we were now in less well-known country, we commenced a regular road traverse, using compass and plane table, taking our distances by perambulator, and making nightly observations for latitude.

As soon as we left Bumban we began to ascend the hills, and before the day was over we found ourselves in a country differing entirely from the coast region. These hills are formed of granite, and are covered with thick bush except on their summits, which take curious shapes, dome-like and columnar. The road is difficult and narrow, and the gradients are so steep that an unencumbered man can only negotiate them by holding on to trees and roots. How the laden carrier manages I cannot understand.

At the end of the first day's march we found ourselves at Kawana, 825 feet above the sea. Continuing to ascend daily we found ourselves, three days later, at Lengekoro, 1500 feet high. The difference in climate now experienced was very noticeable. We had a greater range of temperature; the nights were cooler, the air fresher, and the labour of climbing the hills was more than compensated for by the feeling of increased ability to support fatigue. Within two days of leaving Bumban we recorded an early morning temperature of 66°, and we began to clamour for extra covering at night.

At Kafogo, a village north of Katimbo, three marches from Bumban, we learned that a route existed to Kruto, *viâ* Sandia and Kundembaia, which would save us the circuit to Koinadugu. The head-man of Kafogo, however, said that the road thence to Sandia had not been cleaned, and was impracticable, so we marched on to Lengekoro. At this place a guide offered to lead us to Kundembaia by another route which would save us much, so, on the 30th December, we entrusted ourselves to him, and turned east-

c

ward out of the Falaba road. We found ourselves now passing out of the Limba country into a hitherto untraversed part of Kuranko territory. The road we followed was barely tracked, and led us through almost continuous swamp, and across an affluent of the Seli spanned by a rough trestle bridge, to Kundembaia, a new, clean, and well-built town, where roads from Koinadugu, Lengekoro, Kruto, and Kafogo converge, some of which, however, were not in a practicable condition. The chief and people had never seen white men before, and all the active members of the community disappeared into the bush, leaving the women and the decrepit to face the unknown dangers. As soon as they learned that no harm was done to their belongings, they came in and became very friendly. With little variation this programme was carried out in every town of Kuranko country, except in those near trade routes, where white people had previously been. But the Kuranko were highly delighted with the trade goods we brought, and much edified at the prospect of being protected from their enemies by the white people.

The road we were now following led us into the basin of the Seli river. East of Kundembaia it is in good condition, and following it we reached the river, a fine water, about 60 yards wide and deep, with a rocky bottom and swift current. A most ingenious hammock bridge was constructed here, made entirely of creepers. Three stout creepers, attached to the trunk of a tree on either bank, acted as roadway and handrails, and the space between the handrail and roadway on either side was enclosed by a network of small creepers. The roadway was covered with battens of dried grass, and the bridge was suspended by creepers fastened to the tops of trees. It bore four carriers with their loads at a time. The existence of this very civilized form of crossing at this point is very remarkable, for, as far as we could learn, little or no trade passes through the country, and the towns are only now being rebuilt since their destruction by the Sofas.

From the village of Isaia, near the east bank of the Seli, we ascended the watershed between that river and the Bagwe. The road was bad and the marching very difficult, and when we reached Yerembo, on New Year's day, 1896, our carriers were lying about on the road in varying stages of exhaustion. We got them all in at last, but one was so overcome that he lost his reason and disappeared the next night. From Yerembo we descended next day into the basin of the Bagwe, and halted at Alkallia, a small village, the population of which fled before our arrival, with the exception of an old blind man, who was physically incapable of following their example; but even he succeeded, when we sent for him to question him on the country, in hiding himself. Next day, a very difficult march through more or less continuous swamp, brought us to the Bagwe. The swamps met with in this part of Africa are unlike anything I have met with elsewhere. They consist of heavy stagnant mud, produced, no doubt, by the immense quantities of decaying vegetation, and following the course of the drainage lines which feed the streams and rivers. Where there is a good flow of water, very little swamp is found, and the rivers and large streams had, we observed, almost universally rocky bottoms. The worst swamps are found where there is no water on the surface, and, naturally, no drainage except after heavy rain. The mud is from three to four feet deep, sometimes more, and is often as offensive as if it was the sewage of a city. A hammock-boy carried us over the swampy ground, and as it required great strength and skill to pilot one safely through the heavy mud, each of us selected the most able of his team. In spite, however, of threats and encouragement, we did not pass all the obstacles without some amusing casualties, our doctor in particular, who was no light weight, being on one or two occasions landed by his bearer in a choice position. As soon as the hammock-boy had produced a casualty, he invariably fled to avoid vengeance, and the extrication of the victim was always the worst part of the disaster.

Between Lengekoro and the Bagwe river we experienced every morning a dew-fall so intense, that after five minutes' marching we were as saturated as if we had been exposed to heavy rain. The air was so filled with mist that nothing was visible more than a few yards away. The dew lasted till the sun had been up some time, and it was particularly noticeable during this stage of our march, though there was at all times a considerable mist in the early morning.

We crossed the Bagwe partly in canoes and partly by a ford. It is a fine river, the foliage of the trees on the banks being very beautiful. Its width opposite Kilela, our halting place, is about seventy yards. Kilela is a new town, under a brother of the Chief of Kruto, lying a mile east of the river and a mile or two west of the Falaba-Kruto road. From this place we marched to Kruto, a large town in a low position, with a bad water supply. It is a comparatively civilized place, and has a police barrack occupied by a small detachment of Frontier Police from Falaba, to which place there is a fair road by Koinadugu. The Chief received us with much ceremony, and presented us with a bullock and a considerable amount of rice. His authority extends over a large district and he brought in all his people to welcome us, and executed a dance with them. As I was working outside my hut, taking little notice of the proceedings, I suddenly realized that the mass of singers and dancers, led by the Chief, was bearing down upon me. Retreat was impossible, so I had to resign myself to the situation. The Chief, continuing his song and dance, seized me by the hand and waved it backwards and forwards for some time. I appreciated the honour, but was very glad to escape from the ceremony, and not a little thankful that Captain Tyler, being laid up with fever, could not immortalize me in a humiliating position. The ceremony being over, the Chief sent to me asking for some medicine. I offered him a selection of Burroughes and Welcome's tabloids, but he sent a messenger back to say that what he wanted was medicine out of a bottle, the same as consumed by white people, or, in other words, alchohol. It was evident that this Chief was far in advance of his countrymen in civilization, but I thought it prudent to check his aspirations in this direction. This was the only occasion on which we were asked for drink during our expedition, from which it may be gathered that there is either no trade with the part of the interior visited by us, or that the craving for drink, as it exists in other parts of West Africa, is unknown in these regions.

We observed here first, and afterwards at many other places in Kuranko country, a custom corresponding to that of burying the hatchet in North America. In the centre of the village two guns were half buried in the ground to signify that the war, *i.e.* the Sofa war, was over, and on these various charms were suspended.

The second stage of our march ended at Kruto. The distance recorded by the perambulator from Bumban was ninety-three miles, but the route being very difficult and the country hilly, it took us ten days to cover it. I had intended to halt here one day, but the deep swamp we had recently passed through now began to tell its tale, and several of the Europeans were down with fever. Out of the seven with the British Commission five were attacked within a day or two after we crossed the Bagwe. We were, therefore, reluctantly compelled to remain two days at Kruto, and it was only on the morning of 7th January, 1896, that we were able to start on the last section of our march to the Niger sources. The country we now entered upon becomes more distinctly mountainous than that west of the Bagwe river; the features are larger and the ascents more continuous. In front of us lay a high range terminating in the Kintiballia Hill, on the top of which the Chief of Kruto had his town till it was removed to its present position by order of the Governor. Our route brought us past this range, which we skirted, passing to the south of it. We were now once more off the known routes, but had no difficulty in finding our way to Kurubundo, our next point. Halting at Nyedu and Sogurella, we reached this place three days after leaving Kruto. It is situated on the upper slope of a densely wooded hill in a very picturesque position. A narrow, steep path leads to a war fence, consisting of two massive timber gates, one behind the other, with a very narrow difficult approach connecting them and forming the only way of entering the town. The bush surrounding the town is so dense as to be practically impenetrable, except by this narrow path. The top of the hill is covered with massive granite boulders, and between these the huts are built. The place is a good example of a mountain fastness, where any one inclined to give trouble could take refuge without fear of being dislodged except by a well-organized expedition. It has the reputation of being the only Kuranko town which was proof against the attacks of the Sofas.

The influence of the place was very apparent in the appearance and bearing of the people.

In physique they are decidedly superior to the Kuranko we had met hitherto, whilst it was very evident from their manners that they never forgot the strength of their position. We were met on arrival by the Chief with his people, all of them armed with trade guns and swords. I pointed out to the Chief that his town was situated within the British sphere, and later on I got the French Commissioner to confirm my statement. A flag was given to him and the usual presents were exchanged. I then directed him to remove his war fence. In the meantime one of our carriers had discovered his sister, a Mendi woman, in the town. She was a slave to one of the chief men. I therefore arranged for her release, giving the owner compensation in trade goods to the value of about £2. The woman and her brother were dispatched to Freetown at the first opportunity.

The Chief of Kurubundo, about whom I had some doubts at first, accepted his new position loyally, and proved of great assistance to us later on. We had now arrived at the end of our tether as regards the direction of our further advance. We had no information in which direction the Niger sources lay, or how distant they were from us. We elicited here that there was no road to Tembi Kunda, but the Chief undertook to cut a road for us to the town of Porpor, whence we should probably be able to find a way. All night long his men worked with knives and cutlasses, and in the morning we were able to proceed, and to reach Porpor without any serious difficulty.

As the country adjoining the Niger watershed was believed to be very scantily peopled, it was urgently necessary to reduce our native establishment, which had to live on the country, within the narrowest possible limits. Taking with us a month's supply for the Europeans, and only the stores actually required, all remaining loads were directed on Falaba, to which place also the depot which had been established at a village near Kurubundo was removed. Head-men and Frontier Police were detailed to supervise these operations, on the

# THE JOURNEY

completion of which the natives were to return to Freetown and to be paid off there. By this means we reduced our native establishment to 270 men, but it was impossible to get it lower than this, for the carriage of our instruments, tents, and clothing, as well as our food supplies, took up the services of a large number of men, and the servants and hammock-boys added to the number.

At Porpor, one of our natives, who had been sent on to explore the country, returned to us, having discovered a route to Tembi Kunda. But the Chief of the place, who appeared anxious to do his best for us, told us he knew of a more direct way than that which our man had followed, and provided guides for us the next day. The people of this country have a system of keeping secret from strangers the most direct route between towns, and of sending them round by a circuitous road. Their object appears to be to keep to themselves the most direct means by which they can escape if attacked. To assist them in doing this, the road is often not cut through to their towns, and they reach it by passing through the bush for some distance. We met with many instances of this practice, and it was a sign of the favourable disposition towards us of the Kuranko that we were so often introduced to their private roads. In this case a specially selected head-man of carriers, noted for his walking powers, had been sent to find a way to Tembi Kunda, and the natives had guided him by a road which made him cover twice the distance necessary. Guided by the Chief's men we marched by a different road, and reached Buria on January 11th, where we found ourselves just above the valley of the Bafin river. The Chief of Buria provided us with guides, who next day led us across the Bafin river, which here is a rapid mountain stream about 30 feet wide, and forming no obstacle. We then commenced a regular and steep ascent to Kamindu, a little village, where we halted. On the 13th we continued our ascent, and gradually rose till we stood on the crest of a long ridge running across the track we were following, and having an altitude, on the road, of 3300 feet. Our guide now told us that the valley in front of us was that of the Tembi, the longest tributary of the Niger, and we knew then that we were standing upon the boundary line between British and French territory, the watershed dividing the streams flowing into the Niger from those running westwards into Sierra Leone. Of the valley in front of us little could be seen. The country was clothed with the cane brake, which grows to 10 feet high, and which is such a complete obstacle, both to movement and to observation. Still, we could discern the green foliage, which indicated that a watercourse was there. Our guides pointed out to us the valley, but neither threats nor persuasion would induce them to lead us to the head. Any attempt to force them would only have ended in their lying to us, leading us astray, and escaping at the first opportunity. As a matter of fact, they both disappeared before we reached the valley. In such a country nothing is easier than to step aside into the bush when out of observation for a moment, and to disappear beyond all danger of pursuit. The natives of this country have the greatest dread of the Niger source. They regard it as the seat of the devil, who is the only supreme being they worship, and they believe that to look upon it is to meet certain death within the year. Our visit to the place was regarded as very likely to provoke the evil one into an undesirable form of activity in the neighbourhood, and, in order to prevent this, the inhabitants of the nearest village sacrificed, some days later, a white fowl, and sprinkled its blood on the trees near the upper slope of the Tembi valley.

Deserted by our guides, we forced our way through the cane brake which covered the slope of the ridge. We were now in the Tembi basin, but the actual valley in which the stream ran lay still some way in front of us. At length we reached the green foliage, and, having done so, turned immediately southward and followed the valley till we turned its head. We knew then that we were close to the object of our search. Accompanied by Captain Cayrade of the French Commission, we struck into the valley on the eastern side, and cut our way down to the bottom. This valley, like almost every watercourse in that part of the country, consists of a deep ravine with steeply sloping sides covered with trees, creepers, and bush, and very difficult to penetrate. Cutting our way through the undergrowth, we crept and clambered down the slippery slopes till we reached the bottom, and came to a moss-covered rock from which a tiny spring issues and has made a pool below. The foliage at this spot is green, most luxuriant, and beautiful, and, as one looks on the birthplace of the Niger, it is easy to imagine oneself at a dripping well in some wood in England. The spot is shady, too shady indeed, for sun, light, and air are in the one case altogether, and in the other too much, excluded. The darkness is characteristic of the valleys of this land. The foliage is so dense, and the creepers are so abundant, that the sun cannot penetrate them, and it is probably owing to this, and to the immense quantity of decaying vegetation, that malaria is to be found even in the higher regions of the interior.

In the pool which receives the first waters of the Niger we found a bottle with a note inserted, announcing that Captain Brouet, a French officer, had visited the place in 1895, and on the rock his initials, G. B., were cut. That the bottle was allowed to remain untouched is a proof that no native approaches the place, for in this country a bottle is a highly valued article of trade. A few days later we found some natives with fruit, of which there is very little in this particular neighbourhood, and we brought out all our trade goods to offer them a selection in exchange for their bananas and papaws. After examining everything carefully, and after looking with longing eyes on our cottons and our beads, they eventually fixed their affections on an empty pint champagne bottle, and for this they gave us all the fruit they had. Our

## THE JOURNEY

personal attendants and hammock-boys made no small profit out of the local demand for empty bottles, which were their perquisites, and which they quickly converted into rice, cassava, fowls, or native tobacco.

The natives, amongst their other superstitions, have a great dread of drinking the water of the Niger. Not having any superstitions, we drank it freely, when we visited the source, and not long afterwards were fain to admit that the natives were wiser than we. Indeed, judging from its effects, there is some ground for believing that the river is indeed haunted. Having quenched our thirst, and having attempted to photograph the scene, in vain as it turned out, the light being too bad for our artist, Captain Tyler, we retraced our steps and climbed the side of the ravine. We pitched our camp outside the ravine and west of it, the French being south of us, and the Niger source approximately opposite to the east of the interval between us. Our natives built us a shelter, a square hut covered with banana and other leaves, which was much cooler during the daytime than the tents. They were very expert at this work, and in such a country, where wood to form supports, grass for string, and foliage for covering are so abundant, it is easy to rig up a very decent hut in an hour's time. These shelters, being made with flat roofs, afford no protection against rain, but they are useful against the sun and convenient for working purposes. In the West African climate no one sleeps in the open air; the heavy dew-fall makes protection in some shape necessary. The Europeans of our party used tents, of which the colonial pattern, a double-fly tent, was the most comfortable; the natives improvised shelters, or crept under the low boughs of a shady tree, or slung hammocks in the higher branches. When halting in villages, we usually sent on a head-man to select huts for ourselves, which the owners temporarily evacuated. The native huts are built almost universally on one plan, the only difference being in size, finish, and comparative cleanliness. They are circular in shape, the wall of mud being built up till it reaches the high pitched roof, which is supported by a central pole. The roof is of grass, bound to a framework of sticks, and it projects beyond the wall so as to form a verandah, the ground of which is raised about a foot above that of the interior. There are two doorways to the hut, opposite to each other, and they give the only light to it. The inside therefore is very dark, smoky from the smouldering fire which is always burning, and not too clean. We found it best to quarter our servants in the hut, and ourselves to occupy the verandah, where we could sleep undisturbed even by the hornets and rats which dwelt in the roofs. Later on, when we had accustomed ourselves to our tents, we much preferred them to the huts, and seldom occupied a native dwelling again.

Our camp at Tembi Kunda was found to be 2800 feet above sea level. The highest altitude we recorded was on the watershed just west of the camp, which was 3300 feet above the sea. This point was considerably lower than the tops of the mountains in the neighbourhood, but I think it is improbable that any of these are much more than 5000 feet high. The country as seen from any of the eminences about is decidedly mountainous, much more so than that we had passed through. In every direction masses of upturned granite are to be seen in the form of peaks, columns, and ridges. Toward the south a series of peaks are visible at ranges of from eight to twelve miles; in the neighbourhood of Tembi Kunda, the Konkonante mountain, and the Sulu peaks, two conical mountains side by side, called the brother and sister, are most conspicuous; to the west lies Mount Kenna, and to the north the Kolate range, ending in the Kula peak, a massive column of red granite. The tops, and occasionally part of the slopes of the mountains are bare, but these bare spots are patches amongst the universal high, stiff cane brake aud bush which clothes the whole country. The cane brake and dry bush distinguish the spurs and slopes from the valleys and waterlines, which are easily recognized by the dense green foliage and creepers. The valleys are all deeply eroded, and have steep, rugged sides.

Near the Niger sources there are very few inhabitants, and there is hardly a track or road to be seen. The ruins of a village called Tembi Kunda lie some little way north of the source, and at Konkonante there is a small village, but otherwise there is no sign of human life. In this solitude, however, nature is carrying out a great work. Three tiny streams, all destined to become mighty rivers, commence their journey within sight of each other. Close to the head of the Tembi ravine, and within a very few yards of the spot where our first beacon was built, the Mantili rises and runs away southwards. Its evolution has not yet been traced, but there is no doubt that it is the origin of one of the great rivers which flow into the Atlantic in the south-west corner of Sierra Leone. Half a mile west of its source rises the Bagwe, which we had crossed near Kruto, where it is a fine river. Lower down, after being joined by the Bafi, it becomes the Sewa, a large river, which reaches the Atlantic in the southern part of Sierra Leone.

It was January 13th when we reached the Niger source, and we spent six days in our camp there, busied with observations and survey work. A triangulation was begun, and a base line measured, not without much difficulty, as flat ground does not exist, and the chaining had to be done on broken, hilly, bush-covered country. From the time of our arrival at this place we said good-bye to roads, and worked through the bush, defining the boundary as we went. This was difficult for ourselves, but even more so for the natives, whose unprotected feet and legs suffered much from the strong cane brake and thorny bush. A way had to be cut through the undergrowth, and for this purpose a party of natives was detailed each day to precede us with large knives, or cutlasses as they are called, and to cut or press down the bush to make a way. Our progress in this way was terribly slow, so slow, indeed, as to baffle all calculation. We would spend an hour in climbing a small elevation, which appeared to be within five minutes' distance, in order to view the country; and in surmounting the high ridges and summits where we had observing stations an entire day was taken up in doing what was estimated as a couple of hours' task.

The climate, during the months of December, January, and February, in the elevated country, was by no means insupportable. The difference between the air of this country and that of the coast is marked, and one is undoubtedly able to undergo greater fatigue, and to do more active work in the interior than on the coast. The nights at this time were cold, one blanket at least being necessary, and in the early morning our thermometer several times was as low as 58°. But strangely enough the weather was very inconsistent, the coldest night being followed by a close, hot one, and it frequently occurred that the highest reading of the month was on the day following that on which the lowest reading had been recorded. This, I imagine, was due to change of wind. The harmattan, a hot dry wind from the Sudan, brought the fresher air and cooler nights, whilst a westerly wind from the coast accompanied the close, hot weather. The harmattan is disliked by the natives, its effect being to dry up the skin and congest the membranes, but to Europeans it is much preferable to moist winds from the coast. In the daytime the heat was considerable, but not unbearable, and we found it possible to work all day during these mid-winter months. On the top of the mountains we always found the air to be decidedly cool. This sometimes produced a feeling of chilliness, probably from the action of the dry wind on the moist skin. In West Africa the skin is always moist when the body is at rest, except during fever. When one takes violent exercise, the moisture is not limited to the surface of the body but pervades one's clothing from head to foot, and from inside to outside, giving one the appearance of having emerged from a bath.

Whether the interior is less malarious than the coast is a vexed question. All our party of Europeans suffered from fever at more or less regular intervals, but whether the malaria

# THE JOURNEY

was absorbed during our passage through the swampy coast region or in the higher country I cannot pretend to say. Of swamp as understood on the coast, *i.e.* three or four feet of poisonous smelling mud, there is not much in the high country; but there is marshy ground in abundance, and the valleys are filled with decaying vegetation from which sun and air are excluded. But I must not be led astray into discussing here the always absorbing question of the climate of the West Coast. It will be sufficient to say that our lowest early morning reading between Bumban and Kruto was 58°, the highest 73°, and the mean 68°. The lowest day reading was 68°, and the highest 84°. From Kruto to the end of January the lowest early morning reading was 58°, and the highest 75°, the mean being 69°. The lowest day reading was 67°, and the highest 86°.

# CHAPTER III

## THE WESTERN WATERSHED OF THE NIGER

WE had now been a month in the interior, but our real work was only just about to begin. We had reached the point where the delimitation was to commence, and we set up on the ground at the head of the valley, directly south of the Niger sources, our first beacon, made like almost all those subsequently erected, of a pile of stones in the shape of a sugar loaf. The second beacon was raised on a high ridge north-west of the sources, the ridge forming the watershed, and the third on the same ridge at the point from which we had first looked down on the Niger valley. We placed a beacon at every point where a road or track crossed the frontier.

# THE WESTERN WATERSHED

After completing our preparations for surveying the frontier country, we moved off from our camp at Tembi Kunda on January 19th, following the watershed in a northerly direction. But our progress was slow, and we moved our camp only every alternate day, and then but a few miles. The deserted country lasted for several marches, and then we entered a district fairly well populated, and from that time were never far from habitation as long as we followed the watershed.

Upon the difficulty of following a watershed I need not dwell here in detail; it is well known to those who have had such a task in boundary delimitation to perform. Our difficulty at this stage was not to find the watershed, but to predict its course with sufficient accuracy to judge where our next halting place was to be. I can safely affirm that we did not once succeed in fixing on a good position for our next camp. It was a matter of great importance to us to know in what direction our next move would take us, for we could not naturally drag with us to the top of mountains and to other places which it was necessary to visit for survey purposes, our whole army of carriers and servants, and our whole camp equipage. The wiser course appeared to be to select by eye the position for the day's halting place, to point this out carefully to the most intelligent head-man, and to send on the natives (except those required to cut roads, build beacons, and carry instruments) to pitch our camp and prepare for our reception.

This course had the merit that we were sustained throughout our day's work by the belief that we should find on our arrival in camp our tents pitched, and food, rest, and refreshment prepared for us. But we calculated without allowing for two very important conditions—the one, the vagaries of the watershed; the other, the vagaries of the native mind. The watershed was never where it ought to have been according to our finite judgment. If we expected to find it leading us straight to the front, when we came to follow it, it doubled back and brought us to the rear of our previous position; if it ought to have struck off to the left, it, in fact, took an early opportunity of running away to the right, and led us miles in an unexpected direction. Thus, we generally found ourselves at the end of our day's work far away from the place which we had selected for camping out, and we had the additional task of going there in the afternoon, and of returning next day to take up the work where we had left off. No doubt the proper course in such a case is to examine the ground first before commencing the survey and delimitation, but in our case time was the important consideration, and we could not count on finishing the work before the rainy season set in, unless we pushed on every day, and kept our whole party at the delimitation and survey.

But when we arrived at our camping ground, our dreams of rest and refreshment were rudely shattered. Our eyes vainly searched for tents, baths, clean clothes, food, and drink. Not a sign of them was visible. And yet the spot had been pointed out with great care to the most intelligent of headmen. This happened not once, nor twice, but systematically. We were slow to believe at first that it was not a pure accident which would not recur, but experience of a most unpleasant nature taught us at length that the causes lay beyond our control. It is, perhaps, not to be wondered at that natives, unprovided with shoe leather, find it pleasanter to follow a beaten track than to march through the bush, and it is still less remarkable that they should prefer the shelter of a village to a bivouac in the bush. But whilst admitting these points, we took some time to learn that, unless led by a European, a body of natives moving across country, as soon as they strike a track will follow it utterly regardless of its direction with reference to the line they are ordered to follow, till they reach a village, where they will settle. Ignorance of these principles cost us our breakfast on many occasions.

Starting early after light refreshment, we frequently got no solid food till three, four, or five o'clock in the afternoon. The French officers, more experienced with the natives, and having a smaller and handier following, never let their carriers leave them.

Survey operations were rendered difficult by the impossibility of seeing far in this country. In the morning the dew-fall made the air thick, and in the daytime the haze was very great. Distances, we found, are most deceiving in such an atmosphere. Mountains which appeared to be fifty miles away were barely a quarter of the distance, and our trigonometrical points, which we marked with flags, could not be seen at a greater distance than three or four miles under ordinary circumstances, and the utmost range we ever fixed a point at through the theodolite telescope was probably under seven miles, and in the afternoon. The effect of this haziness was to prevent us from bringing into our survey distant points to our right and left, and from connecting it with known positions in the interior of Sierra Leone.

On January 24th, having made a more than ordinarily false move in search of the watershed, we found ourselves at Bali, a fine town in an interesting hilly position. This place is under the Chief of Kurubundo, and we were pleased to recognize on the lower limbs of the head-man some cotton which had formed part of our present to his master a fortnight earlier. From this town we worked backwards to the watershed, passing several native villages, and finding ourselves in a populated district, of which the principal towns are Kulakoia, Samaindu, and Dandafarra. From Samaindu one day was spent in ascending the high Kula peak, where a cruel disappointment met us, for the haze prevented us from picking up the back station. Next day another mountain was ascended with the same result. Operations at this time were also interfered with by the swarms of locusts which had invaded the country. When they were in flight, a dull red cloud, through which nothing could be seen, obscured the view. When they settled they covered everything, and the ground took a reddish tint from them instead of wearing the ordinary yellow and green of cane brake and bush. We heard them bringing down branches of trees with a crash by their weight. Some scepticism was at first betrayed by some of our party on this point. It required some faith to believe that the breaking of boughs, which often was audible within a short distance of us, was the work of these insects, but we all came eventually to have no doubt about it.

Curiously enough, the natives appear to have no great objection to the locusts in this country. It may be that the amount of cultivation is so very small in comparison with the vast extent of bush, that the crops escape comparatively cheaply. But they have another reason; for, if the locusts eat their crops, they have their revenge by eating the locusts. They catch and preserve as many as they can, and the dried insects form the only meat diet the majority of them enjoy from year to year. We met the locusts from time to time, the last occasion being by the Kita river, where they were being pursued by a large flock of cranes which were dealing with them very effectively, though without reducing their apparent numbers.

The work throughout the delimitation of the watershed boundary was very severe, and during the first ten days its effects were most apparent on our shoe leather. The hard red granite of the mountains played such havoc with our boots that we were soon reduced to extremities, and had to face the prospect of being reduced to go barefoot. Special messages were sent to Freetown for such boots as could be obtained there, but our demands were not supplied till many weeks later, and then the only boots of local construction we obtained were reduced to pulp in two days.

After leaving Bali some days of the severest exertion we underwent during the expedition brought us to Kulakoia, and thence to Samaindu, a place situated in very difficult mountainous country, whence we crossed the Kolate range to Dandafarra, situated on the northern slope. From this place we moved on January 31st to Boria (or Bogoria). As we were finishing a hard morning's work and entering this place, Captain M'Kee, our officer of the Frontier Police, was attacked with heat apoplexy, and in spite of everything that the skill and devotion of Dr. Paris could do, he never recovered consciousness, and died within half an hour of the seizure. Captain M'Kee, who was quite a young officer, only landed in the country a few weeks before the arrival of the expedition, and this was his first trip up country. He was a man of magnificent physique and great personal strength, but the climate seemed to poison him from the first. He had suffered a good deal from fever, and the severe work, in spite of his brave efforts, was more than he could support. We laid him to rest the same evening beneath some cotton trees on the outskirts of the place, and we fenced in his grave with stakes, and placed a cross at the head rudely fashioned from two poles covered with the tin from cases of preserved meat. The French Commissioners, who were at Dandafarra, heard of the sad event too late to reach Boria in time for the funeral, but they came over the moment the news reached them, anxious to be present at the last rites. Boria is situated on the French side of the frontier, and the French officers gave instructions to the Commandant at Farana, in whose district it lies, to see that the grave was respected. It is situated in a spot probably never before visited by white men, and not likely to be much frequented in the future.

We were now on the northern side of the Kolate range, in a country broken and difficult, but less distinctly mountainous than that from which we had just emerged. We marched from Boria to Mussadugu, where Captain Tyler took a lunar photograph, and thence we passed by Kirimandugu and Konkekoro to Kiridugu,

# THE WESTERN WATERSHED 71

where we arrived on 7th January, 1896. This part of the country is the most populated of any on the watershed in Kuranko, and contains many fair-sized towns. Kiridugu, the capital of Mangalia, is the largest town we passed in the interior. It is strange that a prosperous looking place like this can have flourished without any connection with the trade centres on the coast. As far as I could learn it had rarely been visited by traders, and its existence was unknown in Sierra Leone.

The interest taken by the inhabitants of these Kuranko towns in our cotton goods, tobacco, and other wares was great, and the sensation produced by the uncovering and display of our present was quite as great as, and not unlike, that of a party of children at the sudden unveiling of a Christmas tree. Indeed, to witness the delight and excitement of the natives was one of the chief pleasures we experienced on our expedition. The best proof of their appreciation of what they received was the practical use to which they put their presents. At Mussadugu, for example, the Chief immediately after receiving a present, set to work to pick out the threads from a piece of cloth to make sewing cotton, and then cut out and began to work at a suit of clothes which would no doubt make the heart of his nearest neighbour Chief burn with envy. Every man in this land appears to be his own tailor, and every man is more interested in beautifying his own person than that of his woman-kind. The ladies, if they hide in their little-adorned breasts a taste for finery, have few opportunities of gratifying it, for the men invariably annexed and applied to their own use the cottons, ornamented smoking caps, looking glasses, etc., which we presented to the Chiefs. With the exception of a few beads, the women were clad in the plainest way. This may be partly attributable to the comparative poverty of the Kuranko, and I certainly noticed that the women of other people, in wealthier parts of the country, wore more finery and brighter colours; but I am inclined to conclude from observation that the adornment of the male is a necessity, that of the female a luxury. The women, however, card and spin the raw cotton grown in the village farms, and we often spent an hour, when waiting for our breakfast, in watching them. The cotton is carded by being worked up with two roughly made brushes, and it is spun with a clumsy hand-loom, a specimen of which may be seen in any village.

From Kiridugu, which lies in a low position on the upper waters of the Bafi, we passed to Benekoro, and thence to Farama, a town in French territory at the foot of the large isolated hill, Mount Keme. Our route led us round the southern and western sides of this mountain and brought us into Mongo country, a region becoming still less mountainous but no less difficult, covered as it is with dense vegetation. We found ourselves on the north-west of Mount Keme in a camp at some distance from habitations, and whilst laid up with fever here, I was suddenly told by the native clerk that the natives had eaten up all the rice that remained to us and that no more could be obtained in the neighbourhood. Immediate measures were therefore necessary. Every man we could do without for the moment was sent off with his load towards Falaba under the native clerk, whom I instructed to collect and send food to us at once. We had a depot at Falaba, and rice had been collected there for us. Reduced now to a small party we marched to old Karafaia, a beautiful spot hedged round with trees, whose varied and luxuriant foliage made a most picturesque background to our camp, which was pitched on the ruins of a destroyed town. From there we marched to Morifinia on the Bandolo river. The Chief showed great sympathy with our difficulties and anxiety to relieve them; but he told us that the rice crops in the country round had failed, and that his own people had been brought face to face with starvation. Yet such was his anxiety to serve us, that he hastened to bring forth two fowls and a handful of rice, vowing that he would share with us his last meal and cruse. Although we were now in serious difficulties, we could not withhold our admiration for this generous act in giving away almost all the food in the village. Next day however, our doctor, when shooting for the pot a few miles from this village, came suddenly upon a rice farm, on which were stacks of rice containing enough grain to feed a large force for weeks. He inquired from the Chief of Morifinia who the owner of this grain was, and was told that it belonged to a Chief living at some distance away. The doctor retorted that under these circumstances he should take the liberty of helping himself to some of the rice and of compensating the distant Chief. He of Morifinia appeared to regard this as an undesirable proceeding, and a little argument elicited the information that the rice was the property of himself and his starving people. This being the case the doctor had no compunction in annexing a quantity sufficient to supply our expedition for a week, and he set the carriers to work to beat it, the rice being in the husk, and they set to work on the most congenial task they had to perform during the expedition. The Chief was informed that he would be paid, if he came to me at the next camp, whither I had preceded the remainder of the party. He sent two of his men the following day, and I told them that I would only pay the Chief if he came in person. They said he feared to come lest he should be made to suffer for his sins, but I sent them back to tell the Chief to come, and I would give him the value of the rice. But with him the desire of reward, which was not small, was less than fear of the consequences of his deception; he never came, and we left his country with a greatly modified belief in his generosity and liberality. On several other occasions we noticed similar attempts on the part of the natives to conceal their grain stores from us. Their attitude in this respect was a little difficult to reconcile with their evident desire to bargain with us, and to obtain our articles of trade. It may be that they feared we should seize their food supply without payment; it may be that they produce only just enough to satisfy the requirements of

# THE WESTERN WATERSHED

their own people. I am inclined, however, to believe that life in constant dread of being attacked by powerful enemies has produced in them a preference for secrecy and for devious ways. They are, so to speak, always on the defensive, and always anxious to throw inquirers off the scent.

Armed with the rice we had thus obtained, we escaped a serious difficulty. Our main body of carriers, which had been dispatched to Falaba, and which had contributed nothing to our support, was recalled, and we were able to keep them supplied till we reached a better populated region.

After leaving Morifinia, we passed through a gap in a range of hills which crosses the watershed, and halted at the little village of Bonbonkoro. We now emerged on a country which was very little accidented, and which boasted of but a few isolated hills of any size. Small elevations and gentle undulations are the common features of this part, and the watershed is most effectually concealed by a sea of dense foliage. No more difficult country for our particular task of survey and delimitation can be conceived. The absence of conspicuous marks made it impossible to recognize, when we reached their neighbourhood, points observed from a distance, and time after time we had to face disappointment and failure in this particular. Nor did we get any help towards tracing the watershed line by means either of an absence of vegetation or of any peculiarity of the foliage, such as is frequently to be observed in other districts. The whole country was clothed in bush of such a height that it was impossible to say a few yards away whether the ground was rising or falling, and we constantly crossed waterlines without knowing it, and when at last the false direction was discovered, we had to try back and begin again from the nearest point where we could recognize the watershed. Hitherto we had prohibited the native Chiefs from setting the bush on fire on account of the effect on survey work of the dense smoke, but now our only chance of seeing the ground was to burn the bush,

# THE WESTERN WATERSHED

which we accordingly did as we advanced. If the wind was in a favourable direction, after a bush fire had been burning some time, it was possible to get some idea of the drainage of the country, but it was necessary to wait for a day or more to get rid of the intense heat and the heavy smoke occasioned by the fire.

From Bonbonkoro we forced our way with great difficulty through the bush to the ruined village of Boala Karafaia, which the natives were just beginning to rebuild, and from there we came on February 20th to Dakolofe, a good-sized town in Mongo country. The Chief of the country, who lives at Kombili, some distance north of Dakolofe, sent to ask us if we were coming through his town. I told him No, and asked him to come to see us at Dakolofe. He arrived the next day, February 21st, and brought all his people with him and three or four horses, an unusual sight in this country. These animals, which were about 14 hands high and of very poor quality, with a view to creating an impression, he galloped round the hut where we were working till they were all at death's door. After this entertainment he performed a dance in a ring surrounded by his women folk, who clapped their hands, keeping time with his movements.

At Dakolofe our party, which had been reduced to six Europeans by the death of Captain M'Kee, was further weakened by the invaliding of the senior of the sappers, who had suffered greatly from fever, and was quite unequal to the exertions required for survey work. I took the opportunity of reaching the neighbourhood of Falaba to send him with our doctor to that place, from whence a main trade route leads to Freetown. Dr. Paris took him off, and dispatched him thence with a native dispenser, and he reached Freetown, and eventually England, without mishap.

We left Dakolofe on January 22nd. As the three sappers, who passed through the town some time after the rest of the party had left it, were some distance clear of the place, they were followed by a woman, who fell at their feet and implored them to rescue her. She told them, through their interpreter, that she was a Mendi woman, and had been captured and enslaved by a Dakolofe man. The position was a little embarrassing, for the sappers had no precedent for dealing with such a case, and the outraged owner was following his lost property, and came soon on the scene. The corporal in charge was, however, equal to the occasion, and he insisted on the woman and her master accompanying them to the next camp in order that the case might be adjudicated on there. The woman was eventually released and sent to Freetown. It is rather remarkable that the slaves whom we set free were all Mendis from the south-west coast region of Sierra Leone. How they were enslaved and how they came into Kuranko or Susu country I never could make out. When asked about this, the invariable reply was that they were taken during the war. The war referred to always meant the Sofa and Konno invasions.

These wars had nothing whatever to do with the Mendis, who live quite out of the sphere devastated by the Sofas. I can only imagine that the Sofas, having carried off as slaves all whom they did not kill, the Kuranko, by way of making up their deficiencies, had taken every opportunity of filling vacancies in their establishments by carrying off, whenever they had the chance, women of the Mendi tribe, the least warlike of the Sierra Leone natives.

When we arrived at Salamaia, the next halting place, our survey work received a serious check from the simultaneous collapse of all three sappers with fever. Hitherto, we had each of us gone down by roster, and not more than two at most had been disabled at the same time. It was observed that the period elapsing between the first two attacks of fever generally represented the time during which we could count on immunity, so that if, for example, the second attack came three weeks after the first, at each recurrence of this period special precautions were needed.

# THE WESTERN WATERSHED 83

Being left to ourselves, Captain Tyler and I marched on the 23rd February from Salamaia to Songoia Tintarba, sketching the road. From there on the 24th we followed the boundary to the neighbourhood of Kambaia, where we rejoined our main body, and found Captain Blakeney, the officer commanding the Frontier Police at Falaba, who remained with us so long as we continued in his district.

Kambaia is in Sulima territory, and we now at last found ourselves out of Kuranko country. This country has no paramount Chief, but is broken up into many districts, each of which has its own Chief. Some of the districts along the watershed lie across the frontier, and are now cut in two by the delimitation; the main part of them, however, is on the British side. The districts referred to are Mongo, of which the Chief of Kombili is the ruler; Mangalia, under the Chief of Kiridugu; Daldu, under the Chief of Samaindu.

The Kuranko are rather a down-trodden

race, in the main timid and not aggressively truthful. Their character has been moulded by the events of the past decade, in which they have been interested but most unwilling actors. The wave of the Sofa invasion, the great Mohammedan crusade of the Western Sudan, corresponding to the Mahdi's crusade in the Eastern Sudan, has swept their country from end to end, sparing neither age nor sex, cattle nor dwelling. Every one whom the Sofas considered to be suitable for their purposes was carried off as a slave; the remainder, so many at least as could be captured, were slaughtered. Hardly a town in the whole country escaped destruction; except Kurubundo, every town we saw had been built within the last year or two by Kuranko who had escaped from the Sofas, hidden in the bush, and returned when the country was clear. The bones of those slaughtered can be seen at the entry to the large destroyed towns, and even now many natives bear marks of the wounds they received, some having lost limbs, others showing the traces of terrible gashes. But when the Sofas had left the country, the unfortunate Kuranko were not permitted to enjoy in peace the little that they had succeeded in hiding; for the Konno, their neighbours on the east, a people vastly inferior to the Sofas, but a little more powerful than themselves, made night raids upon them, and carried off their movable goods and their women. Having been in this way the prey to their more powerful neighbours for many years past, it is not altogether surprising that the Kuranko hear of the arrival of strangers in their country with feelings of not unmixed satisfaction, and that their first welcome to us was conveyed through the medium of the women and the aged, the men meanwhile lying low in the bush to await developments. When these perceived that robbery and murder were not our trade, and that we were not bringing a war against them, they came forth, and tried to explain their absence on business grounds. A great laugh was invariably raised against them when they were at last compelled to admit that they ran away because they were afraid we should eat them up, and in this the runaways always joined most heartily.

The energetic measures adopted by the Sofas to proselytize the Western Sudan have borne little fruit amongst the Kuranko, for the great mass of the people remain pagans and fetish worshippers of the lowest type. So far as I could learn, their religion is one of pessimism; influenced, perhaps, by the life they have led amongst enemies more powerful than themselves, their highest aspirations are limited to remaining in undisturbed possession of the little they produce for their own use. They have no ideal beyond this, and the object of fetish devices is to keep off the devil from their persons and property. The weapons with which they endeavour to combat the evil one consist of necklaces of beads, small white flags on their houses and haystacks, and various hieroglyphics in their huts. Some one or two of their towns, however, profess the Mohammedan faith, amongst which are Kiridugu, Kurubundo, and Bali. It is very remarkable how far these places are in advance of the pagan towns. Probably their Moslemism is of a low type, yet each Mohammedan place has a school, and all the trade and the prosperity to be seen in the country is in the hands of Mohammedans, who, in moral tone and cohesion, are vastly superior to the pagans. In this country missionary enterprise has done little as yet. The Church Missionary Society works only amongst the people of Sierra Leone proper, but American missionaries have invaded the western part of Kuranko country, and have established a post at Tibabadugu on the Falaba-Kruto road, where they are training the natives as carpenters, masons, gardeners, etc.

The Kuranko are fond of music, and it was seldom that our palavers were not enlivened by some form of concert. The instrument in general use is made of graduated bits of wood fastened by grass strings to gourds. The performer strikes the wood with two drum sticks shod with rubber, and he wears bracelets of iron, which act as cymbals. A sort of chant made up of two or three chords is played, accompanying one or more singers, and is repeated until the audience is more than satisfied.

We did not succeed in collecting many articles of interest of native manufacture. A few musical instruments, bows and arrows, snuff boxes, daggers, and leather whips (used for keeping the women in order), were the principal curiosities we brought back. Other things we saw more particularly in parts of the country traversed by trade routes, but experience taught us that it was cheaper not to burden ourselves with them, but to purchase them first-hand in Birmingham.

In Kuranko country there is very little pastoral property. The Sofas cleared the country of its live stock, and since their departure little has been accumulated. We found a few sheep, and here and there one or two cows. Horses we very rarely saw, but the people told us everywhere that they did not keep horses on account of their poverty, and not because they would not thrive in any part of the country. The French mules never suffered in health, and I believe that there is no reason why horses and cattle should not do well everywhere. There is no appearance of fly in any part of the country we traversed.

The Kuranko are not an energetic people. They cultivate very little, and produce only what is sufficient, or little more than sufficient, for their own requirements from season to season. They have, however, no motive for increasing their production, for traders have hardly been amongst them, and they have had no opportunity of learning what they should turn their attention to in order to obtain the trade goods which they undoubtedly require. In their country the rubber vine is found especially in the valleys of the watershed; but the natives are ignorant of the way of treating it, and do no business with it. The ordinary articles of production are rice, which is the staple food throughout the country, cassava, guinea-corn, tobacco, cotton, and kola nuts. The last are of great value for purposes of export, and there is a great demand for them in the French Sudan. Cultivation is carried on in the most primitive form. A farm is commenced by cutting down the trees and bush to a height of about three feet. This is left to dry, and then set on fire. Cassava is then planted in the ground, the tree stumps and roots remaining undisturbed, and rice is sown over the top. Two crops are produced annually in this way without any irrigation being necessary.

The Kuranko wear their hair in a short tightly twisted pig-tail on each side of the face. Their dress is a form of toga, worn quite loose, with a pocket in the middle, over the stomach. It is generally of native cotton, dyed blue with the juice of the indigo plant, and short trousers of the same material complete it. The weapons generally carried are trade guns and Birmingham swords in those parts where they can be obtained; in other parts, bows and arrows. They seem to make little use of fire-arms, possibly on account of the expense of ammunition, and we rarely heard them discharge their guns. They have a lively fear of the white man's weapons. When I offered to show them the action of a revolver and gun on one occasion, the whole village cleared out.

The people have now a reasonable prospect of living in security from external foes. The Sofas, who under Samory have given such serious trouble to the French for so many years past, and whom our troops under Colonel Ellis met in 1894 to the south of the area of our delimitation, have been driven from the country, and are now in the hinterland of the Gold Coast. The Konno will be kept in order by the frontier troops. The Kuranko, if instructed what to produce, will have an opportunity of acquiring the trade goods they want, and of enjoying them without fear of molestation.

In February the weather was at first not much hotter than that in January, but towards the latter part of the month the sun became more powerful in the daytime. We had three clinical thermometers with us, reading to 112°, and these, though carried inside boxes, and protected as far as possible from the sun, burst, one after the other, during the month of February. Owing to our ordinary thermometer being carried in a box, which was exposed to the sun on the march, and having round it no free circulation of air, the day temperatures we read cannot be regarded as recording the true height of the thermometer in the shade. We noticed that the highest readings were in the evening about 5 P.M. This was due, no doubt, to the box in which the thermometer was carried being exposed to the sun, and to the inside of the box becoming hotter the longer it remained exposed. We made an arbitrary reduction in all day temperatures in recording them, and they are therefore of no great value. Our lowest early morning reading this month was 58°, the highest 74°, and the mean 68°. The highest day reading was 96°, and the lowest 70°.

It is a little remarkable that our highest and lowest early morning readings were almost always recorded on consecutive days. This is probably merely a coincidence, but if the itinerary be examined, it will be seen that in almost every instance a very low early reading was followed or preceded by a comparatively high one. During the months of January and February we had rain on six occasions, generally at night, and in the form of tornadoes, with thunder. We did not ourselves suffer any serious inconvenience from this rain, which our tents withstood well, but our natives were in a much worse case. Their shelters of leaves and branches were useless against the wet, and after a stormy night they presented a miserable appearance in the morning. A few days of rain in the bush would probably have occasioned us serious loss. As it was, bronchitis was prevalent amongst them, and, in the first day or two of camping in the open, we lost a man from this disease. It is hardly to be wondered at that in their thin cotton clothing they were so susceptible to cold and wet. When in a village, crowded into the huts with a wood fire burning and smoking in the middle, they were in the lap of luxury, but in the bush their case was very different. Being naturally predisposed to pulmonary diseases, a life in the bush, with changeable weather, is always likely to occasion sickness amongst West Africans.

# CHAPTER IV

## THROUGH SALIMA AND KAMUKE COUNTRY TO THE KABA RIVER

AT Kambaia, where we arrived on February 24th, we found ourselves in a comparatively populous and cultivated district lying between the two great frontier stations of Falaba and Heremakono. A great trade route, running *viâ* Berea Futambu, connects these two towns; a second trade route runs from Falaba to Simitia, and good roads, as the term is understood in this country, connect Falaba with Kalieri, Berea Futambu with Kalieri, Heremakono with Kalieri, and Simitia with Farana and the French posts on the Middle Niger. A good road also runs from Falaba by Berea Timbako and Kombili, passing just south of Salamaia, to Songoia Tintarba.

Heremakono is a large town, the main gate of entry from Sierra Leone to the French Sudan, and large caravans pass through the place, trading between Freetown and the Middle Niger. It contains a customs post, and a French garrison under a white under-officer. Formerly a French officer was stationed here, but now the only officer in the district is the Circle Commandant, a lieutenant stationed at Farana.

Simitia has also been a point of entry into the French Sudan, and was garrisoned by French native soldiers; but these have now been withdrawn in accordance with the agreement between the Commissioners which I shall refer to later.

Falaba is a large town, the headquarters of a division of the Sierra Leone Frontier Police under a British officer. It is situated in a position unusually bare for West Africa, and about 1600 feet above the sea, and has the reputation of being, for West Africa, a healthy place. Almost all British trade with the French Sudan passes through Falaba, entering by Heremakono or Simitia. On the road joining Falaba and Heremakono we met caravans with ivory, gold, rubber, and calabashes, and on our march up country, in December 1895, we met daily, west of Bumban, numbers of natives from the Middle Niger travelling to Freetown with their produce.

From Kambaia we passed along the watershed, which was very difficult to trace in this part, to Berea Futambu, a large town just within British territory, where we arrived on the 26th February. The 27th saw us at Kalieri, a fairly large town on an affluent of the Koka, with a terribly tainted water supply, from which we suffered during our stay of six days. There is a police barrack here, occupied by a detachment from Falaba. The road from Heremakono to Simitia skirts the eastern and northern sides of the town.

We spent some days at Kalieri making arrangements for the second section of the boundary delimitation, which started on the 10th parallel, a couple of miles north of the place. Having fixed the latitude, we knew that we were close to the termination of the watershed section, and that a short march would bring us to the point where we must turn our faces westwards. Having, therefore, examined the country and roads around, and beaconed the boundary, we dispatched the depot of supplies, which had been originally fixed at Falaba, and which we had drawn to us at Kalieri, to Kondita, near to which place we expected to be in a month. As it was reported that the country along the 10th parallel was uninhabited, we reduced our establishment to the smallest number we could do with. It was necessary to take a certain number of men to carry rice for the followers, but as it took more than three men to carry a full day's ration for the party, we could not bring with us more than seven days' full rations. To secure us from starvation I dispatched a police non-commissioned officer to collect rice in the towns west of Falaba, and to meet us on the Mongo river.

Before leaving Kalieri a large assembly of all the Chiefs in the country round, from

Falaba, Kalieri, Berea Futambu, Berea Timbako, Mussaia, Singunia, Kamba, Sogaria, Kalia, and Sumbaia, came to pay their respects to us, and we held a great palaver under a large cotton tree outside the town. The speeches were of the usual inflated style, and presents were made to us of a ring of gold, one or two cows, sheep, fowls, and rice, which greatly assisted us in the difficult matter of supply. The gold ring was a piece of the ordinary trade gold, which is always beaten into the form of a ring. Twice during our expedition we received a similar present of a gold ring. These Chiefs, living so near to the great trade routes and frontier stations, were used to white faces, and had no dread of us. They looked on our return offering with less of the childish delight of the Kuranko, and more of the trading spirit of the merchant, and I have no doubt made a pretty shrewd guess of the proportionate value of our gift to theirs.

Our observations at Kalieri showed us that we were in latitude 9° 58′ north, and therefore little more than two miles from the 10th parallel, where our first section of delimitation ended. On 3rd March we encamped as near as we could to the spot where we judged the 10th parallel met the watershed, and commenced to observe the latitude. The French Commission arrived on the 6th, and we spent several days in observing, calculating, and working out independently each other's observations, before we could agree upon the exact spot where we were to turn to the west. The point eventually agreed upon is in a low position covered with bush, and the beacon erected there being difficult to find, we put up an auxiliary mark on the top of the nearest hill to direct attention to this hidden mark.

We were now in a country differing entirely from that south of Kalieri, where the ground is little broken and covered everywhere with thick bush. From south of Dakolofe to Kalieri the watershed follows hardly perceptible undulations, and the ground east of it descends very gently to the valley of the Tintarba, which passes east of Heremakono, running nearly due north. Some ten miles or so west of the watershed a line of hills is visible, with a generally north and south direction. But as soon as one ascends any of the hills which rise directly north of Kalieri, and within a mile of the town, a different country is seen. As far as the eye can reach in any direction north of a due east and west line, nothing can be seen but hills, rounded and saddle-backed, having an elevation of not more than from 500 to 800 feet above the intervening valleys, and all covered with vegetation, and showing no bare rock. The hills are small and close together, and as one looks at them, they appear innumerable, and quite unconnected with each other. Their sides are steep and slippery, and beneath the vegetation is a rich friable loam. Bush fires had been lighted before our arrival, and the cane brake had been burned down, so that a good view of the surrounding country could be obtained from the summits. During our passage through this country we saw many such fires, the effect of which was very fine, the whole surrounding country being illuminated at night, and the roar and crackle being audible for miles. It was interesting to watch a fire surround a fine tree, to see the leaves shiver and tremble as the flames penetrated its heart, and to note its shrivelled, miserable appearance when the fire passed on, leaving a smouldering ash in the core of the tree, which continued to burn for days, eventually reducing it to tinder, and leaving nothing but a short, blackened stump, the upper part of the stem being traceable only by the shape and colour of the ash left on the ground.

There is little danger about these fires, as although the heat and the fierceness of the flames are great, their rate of progress is not sufficient to make it difficult to avoid them. On one occasion, however, a tent in which we were breakfasting narrowly escaped being consumed, and we only got it down just in time, the only casualty being a hole in the lining.

The natives require no matches in the interior of West Africa, as the amount of wood available for burning being without limit, some is always kept smouldering, and can be fanned into flame at any time.

So far we had met with little game, and our daily work, from which we could afford to take no relaxation, gave us no opportunity for seeking it. In the cultivated country bush fowl were plentiful, but difficult to get on the wing unless one set oneself regularly to work to surround and beat them. Pigeons were also fairly numerous in the fields, and antelope were now and then put up. On the mountains of the watershed line we saw and heard large apes, but they were timid and would not let us approach them. Monkeys were numerous around the villages. It is quite possible that other kinds of animal life are to be found in this country, for in such dense bush one might pass close to anything without disturbing it.

The second section of our delimitation was to take us westward along the 10th parallel of north latitude to the point where it cuts the Kaba or Little Skarsies river, a distance of about forty-five miles. Time was now becoming a matter of great importance to us,

We could not calculate upon more than six weeks of fine weather, and we had still a large piece of work to be done. Our numbers had been reduced from seven to five Europeans, though we were temporarily reinforced by Captain Blakeney, and sickness might at any moment still further weaken us, or for the time stop our work. The French also had suffered, and their European sergeant had to be dispatched to the coast. In addition to the boundary line, which ended near Wellia on the Great Skarsies, there remained also the Samu frontier, from Kiragba on the Atlantic coast to the Mola river, to demarcate, and on the 9th March Captain Millot left the French camp near Kalieri to meet Captain Sharpe of the Frontier Police at Kiragba on 1st April, and to carry out with him the beaconing of this section of the frontier.

On the 12th of March, having beaconed the starting point of the second section of our boundary line, and having observed a true east and west line, we set off to follow this line in a westerly direction. The advantage of demarcating a boundary along a parallel is that every step you take carries you in the direction of your terminal point, and that there is no doubling back or breaking away to right or left, as in the case of following a watershed. But, on the other hand, the drawback is that you must follow the boundary very closely, and that being a purely arbitrary line, having no relation to natural features, it is certain to take you over some very difficult ground, and you can count on no assistance from roads. Every step we took we had to cut or force our way, and at the elevated positions, where we had to fix and verify our line, much clearing and cutting had to be done. Our advance was always preceded by a party of natives with axes and cutlasses; and when a road was crossed, all our carriers had to lay down their loads and help to build a beacon. Our progress was thus exceedingly slow, the distance covered in the day being from two and a half to four miles. We worked from daylight till dark, only halting for breakfast in the middle of the day. The water in the country we now were passing through flows generally north and south, and cuts our route at right angles. The hills follow more or less the same direction, and we crossed them at their narrowest parts, so our progress was one constant climbing up and down steep slopes.

Our first day's march brought us to Simitia, where, though it took us much out of our road, we halted to find shelter for one of our sappers who was overcome with the sun and a long fast. It is a fair-sized, clean, and well-built town, lying to the south of the 10th parallel. The town and a small piece of country round it were declared neutral for the present, the French having raised a claim to them under former agreements. We spent a day in beaconing off the reserved area, and one or two days in camp at Bibia, to the north of Simitia, where we again observed the latitude and corrected our line. Through Bibia a very good road runs to Sankaran on the east and to Tagania on the north-west. This road is part of the main trade route from

Konakri on the Atlantic, the main port in French Guinea, to the Middle Niger. It is a broad road, and is kept in good condition. We moved on again on the 17th March, passing through a country which is partly under the Chief of Tagania and partly under the Chief of Simitia. We crossed the Koka river this day, a water of no consequence as an obstacle, which runs northward to join the Mongo. West of this stream the boundary passes through a nest of villages dependent on Tagania or Simitia, cutting them into French or English territory with complete impartiality. Leaving these villages on the 20th, we found ourselves in a country deserted by human beings and given up to large game.

We took with us, according to our ordinary plan, guides from the last villages we had passed, but they deserted during the first day's march, possibly from conscientious motives, as their ignorance of the country was unsurpassable, and we had no rice to spare for useless mouths.

We found ourselves now, as we approached

the valley of the Mongo, in a country swarming with game. The tracks of buffalo were everywhere, and their lairs were frequently passed in the bush of the valleys. Elephant tracks were also numerous and unmistakable, and they and the buffalo, which evidently travel like the natives in single file, had made roads at least as good as those made by human beings. In many instances it was impossible to say whether the roads we crossed were game tracks, hunters' paths, or possibly native roads from and to distant towns. The experts amongst our own native followers could not decide this question, so, when in doubt, we beaconed the roads in order to be on the safe side.

The elephant tracks we found generally following the course of the rivers and large streams. These animals move southwards into Sierra Leone country in the rainy season, about May, and return northward when the dry weather sets in in November. At the time we passed through this district they had gone into French territory. From the footprints we saw they must traverse the country in large numbers. Traces of antelope also are to be seen everywhere, and we remarked also those of panther, and, in one case, of a lion. But in the dense bush it is not often that one gets a fair view of any game. We often heard the crashing of branches, but only now and again were able to see what was in front of us. The first time we viewed a herd of buffalo was from a ridge overlooking the valley of the Mongo. The herd had been disturbed by our natives, and Captain Tyler was able to get a distant shot at them, after which they broke away and disappeared, some of them charging through the camp where our breakfast was being prepared, and putting to flight our followers.

The Mongo is a river of about 30 yards' width, deep, but fordable, with a clear rocky bottom, running in an open valley. By the side of this river elephant and buffalo tracks are most numerous, and the bush and cane brake are broken down and cut up with wallowing places and lairs of these huge beasts. This river seems a favourite haunt of large game. It is an affluent of the Kaba or Little Skarsies, which it joins in Limba country.

We crossed the Mongo and encamped on a knoll on the right bank. We had hoped to have met here the police corporal who had been sent south-west from Falaba to collect rice for the followers, but no signs of him were visible. Our position was becoming somewhat critical; the halts at Bibia had resulted in our arriving at the Mongo later than I had anticipated, and with much less food in hand. Nothing could be looked for from local sources till we reached the Kaba river; our sole hope lay in our meeting the policeman and his supplies. It was out of the question to wait on the Mongo; every day's delay made our situation worse. We therefore pushed on, giving the men half a pound of rice daily. It would have given us great relief if we could have killed a buffalo, but, although we had an occasional shot at longish ranges, we did not succeed in bringing one down. Had time been available for shooting purposes, we could hardly have failed to secure some game; but all shooting had to be done whilst delimiting, and we could not attempt to follow the herds we met with, when they left the line we had to follow. The effect of the severe exertion in the heat of the day began to tell on us, and our corporal of Engineers was attacked with sun fever on the Mongo river, and partially paralyzed for some days.

Our day's work was now of a rather monotonous kind; the only change we experienced was that of uphill work succeeding downhill, and downhill uphill. We saw no human beings but our own party, and met with no traces of houses or cultivation. Our expectations were, however, frequently excited by seeing, from the crest of one hill, on another distant crest in front of us, a number of black figures in every conceivable attitude, some standing, some sitting down or crouching, some pointing with outstretched arm, some apparently beckoning to us. As we approached the hill where they were, the attitudes continued always the same, the outstretched arms, the beckoning hands remained just as we had first observed them. The effect was curious and weird; we seemed to be looking upon a dead city, the population of which had been petrified in attitudes which they had once taken up. The explanation of this phenomenon was, however, not long delayed, and was of a much less romantic kind than that supplied by the imagination: the figures were the blackened and blasted stumps of trees which had been burned by bush fires. These fires seem to have travelled far, and we met their traces when at the greatest distance from native dwellings.

A day or two after leaving the Mongo I dispatched a party of three selected natives to push on to Yomaia on the Kaba, to seek for our missing provisions, and to send food to us as soon as possible. They were supplied with rations for three days, and struck off through the bush towards the Kaba. I hoped that they would be able to cover the distance in a couple of days, especially as, not being tied to the boundary, they could use any tracks they might find, and that they would rejoin us in four or five days' time. We kept pushing on daily, but we could now only afford a small cupful of rice to each man. But though receiving merely enough to keep life in them, the carriers behaved very well. They struggled on under their heavy loads, till they could stand up no longer. Many lay down with their burdens beside them, and got through the day's march, resting and walking alternately. Our column under these circumstances was a very straggling one, but it was death to any man to halt too long, or to stray from the track, and so all came on during the day. They suffered much from cuts and ulcers on the feet, but they were far more manageable at this time than when receiving full rations and doing less work.

We continued our monotonous march in this way for a day or two, and at last, after a long day's march, we were cheered by the appearance of mail runners from Freetown. They had been wandering about for some time, had passed through Yomaia, and had struck northwards into French territory, and had travelled in a north-easterly direction till they struck a route crossing the frontier, which by great good fortune brought them close to our camp shortly after it was pitched. Our connection with the inhabited world was now re-established, and we knew we could not be far from native dwellings, and must be approaching Yomaia, about the exact position of which we had been doubtful.

The mail carriers also brought us information that our lost supplies were at Yomaia, where the corporal of Frontier Police was awaiting our arrival. As we had hardly any food left, I sent off two men to order him to meet us at once.

Two more marches completely exhausted our supplies, and on the second day we had nothing to give the natives. Fortunately locust beans were found growing on our route, and with these hunger was staved off. A beautifully marked boa constrictor was killed this day, and was eaten by the carriers after being cooked. Some other snakes, together with a few rats and squirrels, formed an appetizing addition to their menu. Wild honey also was found almost daily during our passage through this country, and was eaten greedily. It seemed to have the almost inevitable effect of giving the natives toothache, as we always had a large number of them with heads tied up and groaning with pain, and our doctor had an active time with extractions. It also caused other forms of aches for which castor oil was the remedy, a medicine which the natives regarded with quite a civilized distaste.

We now were coming into a country which showed signs of being inhabited, and we had passed a farm village and one or two routes crossing the boundary. A long march the day after our direst necessity brought us at last on 28th March close to Yomaia, where we found our supplies, and were once more in the midst of comparative plenty. The native corporal, it appeared, had so little confidence in his ability to find us in the bush, that he preferred to sit still with his provisions in a safe place, and to wait there in peace for those who should survive the march through the bush, rather than to risk himself in a rescue expedition. Fortunately we got through this section of our work without losing a man, which is more than might have been expected. The party I had sent on to seek for our supplies got lost in the bush, and the men strayed in different directions, and were nearly starved. All, however, eventually rejoined us.

Yomaia is a good-sized town, made up of three separate villages. It lies about half a mile on the French side of the boundary, and about two miles east of the Kaba river, which we struck the next day, March 29th. We fixed our camp on the high ground overlooking the river valley, and spent a day or two in astronomical observations, and in preparations for our next move. Our police officer, Captain Blakeney, left us here and returned to his station at Falaba.

This second stage of our delimitation had brought us through the Sulima and Kamuke countries, which are now cut in two by the boundary. We also just touched a small piece of Hure country, near the little village of Herako, where a few fields are cut into British territory. The exact division of these countries in the part we passed through it is impossible to define, for we had no guides for the greater part of our march, and when we obtained natives to show us the way, their ignorance of the country was complete. The district is traversed by hunters, it seems, but by no one else. What the hunters get it is difficult to learn. To tackle elephants with trade guns must require considerable courage and great faith, and we could not hear of any ivory passing to Sierra Leone from this neighbourhood. But there is no doubt that hunters go there, and I imagine that they limit their sport to the buffalo and the antelope. We saw in places traps set for the latter, consisting of a loop formed by bending down a strong creeper, which was made into a running noose, and was intended to catch antelope by the neck. Another form of trap in occasional use is a pit covered with light foliage, and made at a place where antelope are likely to go. Our own natives more than once caught antelope, which had been disturbed by our camp, and, becoming confused by the number of people about, were easily captured. These antelope, which are of a red colour, and rather less in size than the black buck of India or the spring-bok of South Africa, are very common in this part of West Africa, and make excellent eating.

The Kaba river, or Little Skarsies, as it is called in Sierra Leone, must be a splendid water in the rainy season. It runs in a valley about a mile broad, with banks from 900 to 1000 feet high, as measured by aneroid, and so steep and broken that they can only be climbed here and there. In the dry season the river is about 100 yards wide near Yomaia, fordable with difficulty, and it runs in a rocky, sandy bed, the water being clear, though the current is very slight. Fish are plentiful in the river, and our half-starved carriers, as soon as they could find a way to the water, which was by no means easy, set to work to replenish their larder. They used, in the first instance, a leaf which drugs the fish and renders them an easy prey, but later they found a much more successful method was to fish at night with a lantern and a cutlass. The lantern caused the fish to rise and with the cutlass it was decapitated.

Guinea-fowl were also plentiful in the river valley, and we heard them daily, but never succeeded in getting them up.

Our next task was to follow the river southwards till we found a point on the western bank four miles south of the 10th parallel. Owing to the broken ground this was not an easy task. We accomplished it by making a small triangulation down the eastern bank, and on April 2nd we fixed a point on the western bank by this means, and camped on ground very little above the river bed, having a height of 750 feet above sea level, the height of the banks of the river at our last camp being 1550 feet.

As we crossed the river and moved along

its valley we found many traces of elephant and hippopotami, and we had not been long in the valley before the appearance of a hippopotamus in the water caused considerable excitement and brought out our five Europeans armed with Martini-Metford carbines, and the native police with their Sniders. A fusilade followed as intense as that of a modern battlefield, and as resultless. The hippo came to the surface about once every five minutes with a snort which made all the natives take several steps in the direction of the camp, and exposed his head for half a minute. During this time a terrible fire was poured into him, but down he went, and up he came again when his five minutes had expired, with unwearying regularity and apparently without being influenced in the least by the shooting. Once, indeed, he attempted to go ashore on the opposite bank, but thought better of it when his whole carcase was exposed to fire, and returned to the water to continue his regular five minutely rise. When the sun set this programme was still being carried out. It was confidently expected, however, that in the morning we should meet with the carcase of the hippopotamus, but whether he had taken in so much lead as to have lost his buoyancy, whether the result shows the defects of the Lee-Metford bullet, or whether it was due to other causes which did not at the time appear to us to have any weight, it is impossible to say, but we certainly never saw anything of the animal again. Two days later the native police sergeant, who certainly shone more as a shot and sportsman generally than in any other rôle, killed an enormous hippopotamus a little higher up the river. The carriers set to work with a will to haul the carcase out, and we soon had an unlimited quantity of meat available. For three days the men gorged at the rate of 4 or 5 lbs. a day, till all was finished, or till they had as much as they could stand. Our camp was meanwhile rendered unpleasantly fragrant with the smell of hippopotamus meat, which was hung up everywhere. This meat has the credit, according to some people, of being very palatable. None of our party, however, had the courage to taste it, but we inquired of those of our boys who had eaten an enormous amount, if it was good. They told us they didn't like it. It may be, however, that they had not given it a fair trial, or that, after their recent fast, they were not in a condition to appreciate delicacies; anyhow, though prejudiced in favour of their view, we could not but regard them as tainted witnesses.

In addition to the hippopotamus and fish we got here also one or two flintambo or waterbuck, a small animal not much bigger than a hare.

During this time we managed to collect a little rice in the neighbourhood of Mandea, and of Kondita. Our depot was at the latter place, and we now took steps to remove it to Yana. Mr. Parkes had also, before we left Freetown, formed another depot of supplies at Kukuna, and we brought up the rice from there to meet us on the next section of the delimitation.

During the month of March the weather

had become decidedly warmer, and we found it told on us during each day's work. Our lowest early morning reading was 63°, and the highest 76°, the mean being 72°. The highest day reading was 95° (a deduction having been made on account of the method of carrying the thermometer), and the lowest was 73°.

The air this month was more charged with moisture than in the previous months, and at the beginning of the month, when near Kalieri, we had some rain and cloudy skies for several days. The rainy season in the interior begins earlier than on the coast, and it was probably near in March. As we travelled westward the skies cleared and the symptoms of rain disappeared. We had in all four days of rain during the month. The exertion was now beginning to tell on all ranks, and it was evident that our party were getting a little stale. The natives, too, broke down in numbers, and we had to part with many of them. Although they had behaved beyond our expectations during the period of starvation and extra work, when the strain ended, many were glad to get home, and all showed much anxiety to bring the expedition to an end. It was now the 3rd of April, and though the rainy season does not set in generally till May, we might expect tornadoes at night with more or less regularity throughout the month. In these parts the rainy season is always ushered in and out by these nightly storms, which last for about a month before and after the regular rains. The natives dread this weather in the bush, and we had, on that account, some anxiety about completing the work, without causing them serious suffering.

## CHAPTER V

### FROM THE LITTLE TO THE GREAT SKARSIES

OUR next section of boundary work involved a task of considerable difficulty. We had to delimit a straight line between the point on the western bank of the Kaba or Little Skarsies, which we had just fixed, and the junction of Kita and Lolo rivers. The position of this junction was known only in a very general way, and it was not possible to tell what the exact direction in azimuth of the line would be. We had hoped to have been able to align flags between the two points, which were some eighteen miles apart, but we at once recognized the impossibility of this on seeing the country. It was very similar to that we had just passed through, very broken, densely covered with bush, and, though very hilly, it contained no commanding ridges from which the ends of the line could be seen. We agreed with our French comrades, therefore, that the best course was to send on two officers to delimit a line taken from the map we had, to see where this line struck a meridian through the Kita-Lolo junction, and from these data to work out a corrected bearing which we could then delimit. Accordingly, Captains Cayrade and Tyler left the Kaba on April the 4th, following a bearing we had taken from the map. We sent our sappers round by road, *viâ* Kondita, at the same time, to push on to the junction of the two rivers, and to erect a beacon there. The doctor and I were left on the banks of the Kaba for six days, and we spent there the dullest time of any during our expedition, for it was possible neither to work nor to leave the place for purposes of sport. Every moment we expected news from Captain Tyler, and our available time was now so short that not a day could be

# THE GREAT SKARSIES

spared; we must move the moment we received his report.

It arrived on the 9th, and we learned from Captain Tyler that he and Captain Cayrade, following the bearing given, had struck the Lolo about a mile and a half south of its junction with the Kita. The exact difference in longitude had been determined by triangulation, and a corrected bearing worked out. Captain Passaga and I set out on the 10th of April to follow this. The country we found very similar to that we had just traversed; it is very broken and hilly, and covered with very difficult bush. The heat was now very trying, and the labour of fighting through the bush to reach the crests of the hills crossed will not soon be forgotten. This country, like that along the 10th parallel, is covered with soil and vegetation, but detached pieces of the red laterite, so common at Freetown, are to be seen everywhere. The hills, though not high, are less rounded than those we had noticed along the parallel, and the ground is more irregular. The highest point we reached was about 1500 feet above sea level, the valley of the Kaba being about 500 feet high. The country is very sparsely populated. We passed near one or two small villages, and there are one or two larger towns in the district, but they lie at some distance from the boundary.

At the end of the third march we came to the edge of a plateau, and descended a very steep slope to a comparatively flat region about 800 feet above sea level. On the 13th April we moved through a flat, bushy country, and crossing the Numelo, a river about 50 yards in breadth which joins the Lolo some miles below its junction with the Kita, we reached the Kita-Lolo junction in the afternoon, and found we were then not more than 600 feet above the sea. Both the Lolo and Numelo run in open flat country, and have low banks. The Lolo is about 75 yards wide, and is fordable at places in the dry season. It has a rocky bottom, and fish are plentiful in it. The

# THE GREAT SKARSIES

Kita is quite a small stream, not more than 10 yards wide.

Our bearing, as corrected by Captains Tyler and Cayrade, brought us accurately to the junction of the two rivers, where the next stage of our delimitation ended, and we put up a large beacon on the eastern bank of the Lolo opposite to this point.

Throughout the march from the Kaba to the Lolo river we continued to find plenty of traces of large game, and on the 12th of April a piece of ivory, the end of an elephant's tusk, was picked up. Antelope were numerous, and we saw buffalo several times.

Our next task was to find a point on the western bank of the Kita, 1500 metres above the village of Lakhata. From the Kita-Lolo junction to this point the river Kita forms the boundary, and therefore no delimitation is required. We set off on the 15th April for Lakhata. Crossing the Lolo and Kita we cut through the bush along the right bank of the Kita, till we struck a road which we followed to Lakhata. We passed several small villages on the way before reaching this place, which is a poor badly built village in a flat country near the right bank of the river. It was under the Chief of Yumboya, but is now severed from that place, which is on the French side of the frontier. The country between the Kita-Lolo junction and Lakhata is almost quite flat, and covered with bush.

Our sappers had preceded us to Lakhata, and had measured with a chain 1500 metres along the river, north of the town. We moved our camp to the place so fixed on the 16th, and set up a beacon there.

The country here once more changes entirely. At Lakhata we were in a flat, low region, covered with a tall dry bush, and between 650 and 700 feet above sea level. North of the village, on both sides of the Kita, the mountains of Tamisso push out towards the south some high, bold spurs, with very steep sides, which terminate abruptly, and tower over the flat country south of

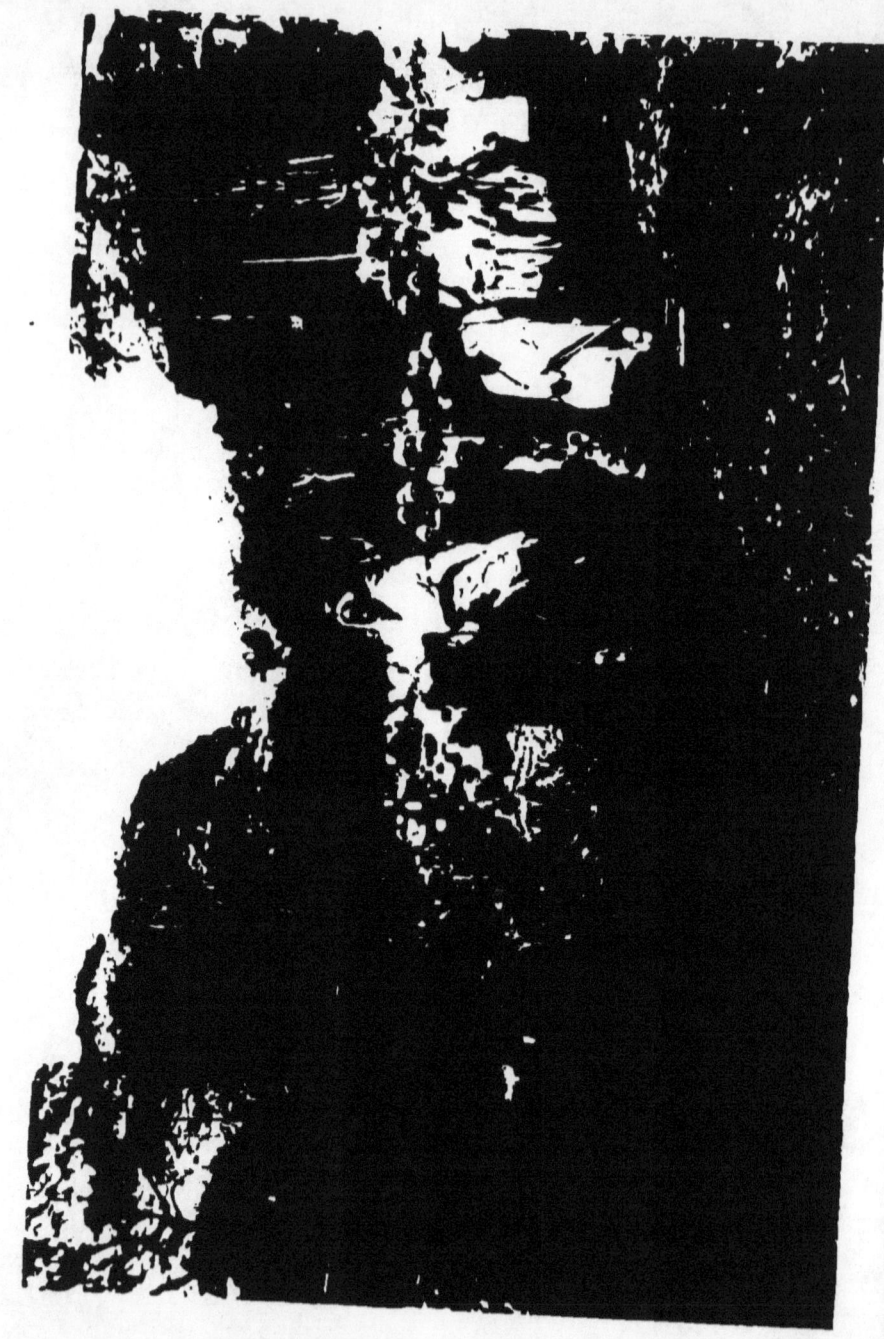

Lakhata. Though following the bed of the river, and therefore the most gradual ascent, we rose 600 feet in the 1500 metres. The river at this point is still falling rapidly, and it descends by a series of cascades a height of 600 feet in about half a mile. We attempted to get a good view of the falls, but they were very difficult to get at, and the view was so much obscured with creepers that the water was almost concealed. There is no single fall of any very great height, but the river descends by successive leaps of 30 or 40 feet, and, where visible, the white spray makes a pretty background to the trailers and foliage.

From the point we had now fixed our next move led us directly across a number of the spurs of mountains of Tamisso. We had hoped that our difficulties were ending, but the outlook was now less promising than at any time. The line had to be directed on to the centre of a gap in the westernmost spur, and the first business was to find this point. Captain Cayrade had been sent to the front to seek for the gap, and, after some days' absence, he reported that the only place like it lay in a direction within five degrees of magnetic west from our beacon. We therefore settled to follow this bearing to see where it would bring us, and made our preparations accordingly.

During our journey, with the exception of the hippopotamus meat, our carriers had seldom tasted flesh. We had but seldom seen cattle, and then only one or perhaps two head at a time. But now great excitement was created in our camp by the appearance, some miles off, of large herds of cattle being pastured on the mountain slopes.

The cattle, we learned afterwards, are the property of the Fulas, a race of shepherds and cattle owners from Futa Jallon in the French Sudan. A party of Fulas were staying at Yumboya, which lies on one of the Tamisso mountain spurs, and were pasturing their herds in our neighbourhood.

We halted four days in this neighbourhood awaiting the reconnaissance of our next objective, and moved off to cross the spurs on April 21st. Our first day's march led us into ground lower than that above the banks of the Kita, and only 1250 feet above the sea. We had at this place some little difficulty with our carriers, who were now getting, relatively speaking, a luxurious diet. Beacons had to be erected, but, this duty interfering with cooking, the boys became somewhat mutinous, and refused to work. When the chief culprits were led forth to be punished, the other natives refused to assist when ordered, and we were in danger of experiencing a strike in the bush. But our doctor, who, in addition to his other duties, managed the transport, nipped this spirit in the bud by the adoption of vigorous measures, and the men were at once obedient and submissive.

On the 22nd April a long climb brought us to the top of the highest spur, and at the village of Kunsi, which lies just within French territory, we found ourselves 2800 feet above the sea, on a broad flat spur in an open country covered with short herbage. This is one of the finest, and certainly one of the pleasantest spots we met with in the interior. The sight of open, flat, level ground, clear of undergrowth and easy to walk on, was very comforting after the eternal bush and the cramped view. The top of each spur is a plateau of many hundred acres of hard, level grazing ground. The formation is a brittle schist, lying horizontally; good water is abundant and clear, and the country is evidently well suited for cattle. Around Kunsi large herds were being pastured, and we obtained, in the village, bowls of excellent milk, a luxury met with here for the first time. Antelope are very plentiful; the French officers, who went out shooting in the afternoon, bagged several with shot-guns. The air was noticeably fresher here than in the lower country, although the sun was now hot and the skies were charged with the moisture of the coming rains. For an interior station this part is probably the best that could be found within the Protectorate from the point of view of health and comfort. Kunsi stands high;

it is free from swamp, decaying vegetation, and bush; it commands a good view, good water, and fresh air. The part of the spur south of the village which falls into British territory is very extensive, and from the southern edge of it the towns of Dumbaia and Saionia are overlooked.

On the next day we moved on across this spur, and having reached the western side, descended by a steep track into a deep valley clad with forest. We crossed this valley, and climbed the next and last spur, finding ourselves at the village of Kankuya, 2350 feet above sea level, and some 450 feet below the spur we had just quitted. This spur is generally similar in character to that on which the village of Kunsi is situated, but not so flat. From its western edge, which is exceedingly steep and in most places precipitous, we could see the plain country beneath us, and the many villages, whose names we identified with the assistance of guides. We could also trace the outline and extent of the spur we had camped on the previous day. These hills are very remarkable features in a country which is otherwise as flat as a billiard table, and they are specially remarkable on account of the steepness of their sides and the abruptness with which they terminate.

Our azimuth line, which we had followed from the Kita, led us to a very peculiar rock, like a perpendicular column, standing at the western edge of the spur, and known as the "rock of Kankuya." This Captain Cayrade had taken for the gap described in the Treaty, which was the point on which our line was to be directed, having failed to find any other form of gap, and not unnaturally taking the word, which was represented in French as *brêche*, to signify a geological fault. But it was clear that this was not the place which the Agreement referred to, though it was not possible from the top of the spur to say whether the gap existed or not. We therefore proceeded the next day, and descended the western face by a very precipitous path, arriving in the plain near the village of

Dantumaia. We then examined the face of the spur, and soon discovered that it was unbroken; no gap existed in it. We had, therefore, to make an arrangement with the French, and to select another point, as nearly as possible in the position referred to in the Agreement, to take the place of the missing gap. We adopted the rock of Kankuya as the terminus of the line from the Kita, and from thence drew the line to another point arbitrarily selected on the westernmost spur.

We had now from this last selected point to draw a line towards a point on the Kora river till it met the great French road from Wellia to Ula. This was comparatively easy to do, the country, though flat, being not so densely covered with bush as in other parts.

We were now in a comparatively well cultivated and populous region; there are here many villages and some largish towns. Our height above sea level was 580 feet; we had dropped 1770 feet during the day's march, and 2220 feet since leaving Kunsi. Before us lay the valleys of the Kora and Kolinte or Great Skarsies rivers, which unite west of Ula; south of us was a plain which extended to the sea. We were once more in the coast region, and the air made us unpleasantly aware of this circumstance. It was heavy, and charged with the moisture of the rains, which were now very soon to break.

We encamped near the village of Balifilli, and found ourselves there on the great French road to the interior, which, starting from Konakri on the coast, crosses the Great Skarsies near Wellia, and passing through Ula, Fodea, Balifilli, Dunia, Wossu, approaches the boundary again at Tagania and Bibia, near Simitia, and runs thence to the Middle Niger.

On the following day we continued our delimitation to Ula, near to which place the line is intercepted by the great road. Ula, which lies in French territory, is a large, important, well-built town, with a customs station, superintended by a white official, and barracks with native soldiers. It is a port of entry for goods passing from Sierra Leone to French territory. The huts are larger, better, more elaborately, and more pretentiously built than any we had hitherto seen; the people are evidently prosperous, and we were fairly struck with wonder to find both a carpenter's shop and a store.

As luxury and refinement of this description was likely to prove a dangerous snare for our carriers, we pushed on in the afternoon. From the point where the boundary approaches the main road near Ula, it is drawn parallel to this road and 500 metres east of it as far as the Great Skarsies river. We therefore followed the road and reached the river, and with it the terminus of our demarcation work in the evening.

Our camp was pitched on the eastern bank of the Great Skarsies, which is here about 100 yards wide, deep and unfordable at any time. It runs in an open, flat country, and has low banks. Hippopotami are found in it in numbers; Captain Passaga succeeded in killing one during our stay on the banks. The river is crossed by a dug-out canoe, by means of which travellers are ferried over. West of the river, in French territory, the ground rises, and hills are visible a few miles away.

From this place we could clearly see the hills of Tamisso, which we had lately crossed, and could trace the appearance which evidently gave rise to the impression that a gap existed. Seen from this distance there is apparently a passage through the face of the hills. This appearance is due, as we saw by examining the spurs, to the projection of one spur beyond another.

On the 26th April the French Commission reached the river, and we now set ourselves to draft the *procès verbaux* of the delimitation, and to complete our knowledge of the neighbouring country. A beacon was erected on the east bank of the Great Skarsies, 500 metres south of the point where the road meets the river, and a similar beacon was placed on the west bank, as south of this point, although the river forms the boundary, it is altogether British.

## THE GREAT SKARSIES 141

Shortly after our arrival at the Great Skarsies we were delighted to hear that the party which had been sent to delimit the boundary in Samu had completed its task, and was on the march northward to join us. This was highly satisfactory news, as we now could complete all the *procès verbaux*, and the description of the boundary and beacons, before leaving our camp. On the 28th the party, consisting of Captain Sharpe, of the Frontier Police, and Captain Millot, the French Commissioner, arrived, having travelled north by the western bank of the Great Skarsies. They had been at work since April 1st, and had had a very difficult task in tracing the watershed between the Great Skarsies and Melakore rivers through a low, bush-covered country. Their work commenced on the Atlantic coast at Kiragba, and ended at the source of the Little Mola river. This river joins the Mola, which empties itself into the Great Skarsies, and the boundary, after following these streams to the junction of the Mola with the Great

Skarsies, runs up the right bank of this river as far as the point where we were erecting a beacon. The delimitation was, therefore, now complete along the entire Anglo-French frontier, for it was naturally unnecessary to take any steps to mark the boundary along the river, where the river itself was the boundary. We had only to complete and sign our documents before breaking up for the coast.

I was greatly astonished, when the Samu party joined us, to observe with them the French sergeant, who had been sent from Heremakono to the coast in order to take passage for France. This man, who had served in the French Congo, had been some years abroad, and had suffered severely from the climate. He had more than once been attacked by a form of sunstroke, and seemed to be in such a serious condition that the only chance of his recovery appeared to lie in getting him on board ship without delay, and he was, in fact, sent to the coast with this object. Yet here he was back again,

# THE GREAT SKARSIES

looking quite recovered, and doing his work as usual. I expressed my surprise at his return as he came up to salute me. He told me that it was entirely due to the sea; he regarded his last expedition as a visit to the sea-side. Kiragba is, however, not exactly an ideal watering-place; it is a low-lying, mangrove-fringed spot, and has the reputation of being as choice a locality as any on the West Coast for swamp. The party had spent several days in wading through its muddy rice lands, and it was undoubtedly a pleasing novelty to hear it spoken of as a health resort.

On the banks of the Great Skarsies game is as plentiful as anywhere in the country. The smaller antelope were numerous and very tame; they would stand watching us at a distance of thirty or forty yards. Our police sergeant shot a splendid specimen of the kudu with a magnificent head. The second night after our arrival in the camp a troop of five elephants, travelling southwards into Sierra Leone, the rains being about to commence, came into our camp, and passed through in the early morning. Our boys watched them, and afterwards described to us in a state of frenzied excitement the length of the tusks of the principal male, and the way he reclined against a palm tree. We followed them ourselves, Captain Tyler with his camera; but they had been alarmed, and travelled fast down the river, leaving enormous foot-marks in the soft ground.

The rains were now beginning to threaten, and on the night of the 27th we had a heavy fall. Next day this was repeated, and rain fell in torrents all the afternoon and night. Our camp was converted into a swamp, and we thought it advisable the next day to move into the village of Wellia, which is about a mile west of the river and about 200 feet above it. Here we completed our documentary work, signed the *procès verbaux*, and, after having been hospitably entertained by our French comrades, we left on May 1st, the French officers accompanying us to the bank of the river, which we crossed in a canoe.

Our followers were all eager to get back to the coast and to receive their pay, which on these occasions is always retained till they are discharged, and they stepped out with a will, and we soon had placed a considerable distance between ourselves and the last scene of our labours.

During the month of April the climate was increasingly trying, and the air full of moisture. Our lowest early morning reading was 70° and the highest 84°, the mean being 77½°. The highest day reading was 100° and the lowest 86°. Rain fell on eight days, the fall on two occasions being very heavy. Still we were fortunate in avoiding the tornadoes we had expected this month, and our followers did very well on the whole. During the worst rain they managed to shelter in a small village near the camp.

# CHAPTER VI

## RETURN TO THE COAST AND EMBARKATION FOR ENGLAND

OUR objective was now Kambia on the Great Skarsies river, where we had arranged to meet a boat from the Governor's yacht, the "Countess of Derby." The distance to this place was about seventy-five miles, and it was important that we should cover it as soon as possible, lest we should be caught by the rain. We marched along the road to Ula as far as the ruined village of Lusenia, and turned off there for Saionia, where we arrived in the morning. Saionia is a good-sized Mussulman town of about 55 houses, well kept, and looking fairly prosperous. After halting for breakfast, we pushed on in the afternoon, and halted at Fodea, a small village in bad repair, the total distance covered being twenty miles. We found no difficulty now in getting our carriers along; they were all so eager to reach the coast that no distance was too great for them.

Next day we marched to Kufuna, a distance of about ten miles, and halted at a poorly-built village. We met here messengers from the Governor announcing that the yacht was awaiting us at the mouth of the Great Skarsies, and asking for information of our whereabouts. We received also a most welcome present of bread, a luxury we had not seen for months, and fruit.

On the next day, May 3rd, we marched in the morning to Berikuri, a large Mussulman town, and in the afternoon to Kukuna, a town of considerable size, covering a large space of ground. We now found ourselves in a very populous country, and on our next day's march to Pettifu, a distance of twenty-four miles, we passed a large number of towns of a good size, the inhabitants of which are all Mussulmans. The country is much cultivated, and really good service has been done by converting a large extent of mangrove swamp into rice fields. At Pettifu, where our last night ashore was spent, the carriers, in spite of their long march, spent half the night singing and dancing to the music of tom-toms. I addressed them through the chief head-man, and informed them that, on account of the good work they had done, all fines, of which a large number had been registered, were cancelled, and I thanked them for their services. Their gratitude was boundless; many of them crept up to me on their hands and knees and embraced my boots, and songs and dances of an uproarious nature followed.

On the 5th May we marched on, passing towns every mile or so, to Kambia, a large place on the river where a considerable trade is done, canoes passing between it and Freetown. We had an interview with the Chief, who was anxious that we should stop, but we had to embark before the tide turned, and so continued our march to Massama, where we met the "Countess of Derby's" gig, which rowed us to Robat, the highest navigable point. Here we were met by Captain Compton, the commander of the yacht, and embarked. Our carriers had started early from Pettifu and marched to Robat, and the loads were all on board when we arrived. One of our party, Captain Sharpe, was now missing. He had remained at Kambia, which was in his police district, to transact some business, intending to follow us. After waiting some time, he sent word to say that he was laid up with fever, and could not come. The tide was now beginning to ebb, and just at this time one of the sappers was prostrated with sunstroke, so we decided to push on, leaving the apothecary to look after Captain Sharpe, with instructions to bring him on next day.

The country we had passed through after leaving Wellia is perfectly flat, there being only one small rise, between Saionia and Fodea, of not more than 100 feet. From the Great Skarsies near Wellia to the same river at Massama, a distance by march of nearly eighty miles, the difference of height as recorded by aneroid is not more than from 110 to 120 feet. The ground is hard, flat, and in many places covered with short herbage, and suitable for grazing. There is hardly any indication of swamp, except on the creeks and inlets of the river, the banks of which are covered with a deep, rich mud. The road is good, hard, very easy, and much straighter than in the more thickly bushed country. There is no appearance of hills on the east of the Great Skarsies, and no indication of a well-marked watershed between the two great rivers, the Great and Little Skarsies. These two large waterways must run through a level plain at a distance of not more than twenty miles apart, separated by no obstacle, and a very little effort would divert the water of the one into the channel of the other.

Before leaving Wellia, the depot of supplies which had been established at Yana, to which place it had been moved from Kondita, was brought down to Kambia by natives supplied by the Chief of Yana, and was embarked before our arrival. We thus found ourselves complete on the "Countess of Derby," and brought back with us everything that remained of our supplies and stores. We reached Freetown late on the night of May 5th, and disembarked on the 6th, when our natives were paid off and discharged.

Two days later I went to stay with the Governor, Col. Cardew, C.M.G., who with Mrs. Cardew was occupying a country residence at the extreme point of the Cape, formed by the Atlantic coast where it is joined by the southern bank of the Sierra Leone river, some seven miles west of Freetown. I remained there till the 12th May, the day before we embarked for England.

Whilst our boundary delimitation was going on, Col. Cardew, who has devoted much time to exploring the interior of the colony, and to questions connected with the politics of the different tribes, made a most important expedition. Accompanied by Major Grant of the Royal Engineers, an officer of a high reputation as an astronomical observer, he followed the Anglo-Liberian frontier from

Tembi Kunda to the point where it cuts the Mano river. This frontier joins the Anglo-French frontier at Tembi Kunda, and starting from the first beacon we had set up at the head of the Tembi ravine, runs along a parallel of latitude drawn through the position of the beacon till it meets the 13th meridian west of Paris (longitude 10° 40′ west of Greenwich). It then follows this meridian southwards till it cuts the Mano river, which forms the boundary thence to the sea. The Governor followed this boundary as far as the Mano river, and explored the very important territory which falls within the British sphere. He fixed in passing the position of Waima, where the unfortunate collision with the French troops occurred in 1894, and which is now proved to be in British territory. The work done during this exploration has contributed a great deal to completing the knowledge of a most important part of the interior, and one which promises to become very valuable to the colony in the future. The Governor's expedition suffered the same fatality as ours: Captain Boileau, the police officer attached to it, whose headquarters are at Panguma, was taken ill on the return of the expedition, and died after an attack of fever lasting a few days. This frontier police force work is evidently very trying, and the rate of mortality is very high. Out of seven officers, in a period covered by less than a year, three died and two were invalided to England. The causes of this serious state of affairs are, I imagine, not only and not even mainly the unhealthiness of the climate, but more particularly the difficulty of obtaining the common necessaries and the common comforts of life in the interior. Except rice, fowls, a little fruit, and occasionally a sheep, everything must be transported from the coast, and the cost of bringing up luxuries is so great that they are quite beyond the reach of those living in the interior under present conditions. But I shall revert to this matter in a later chapter.

During my stay with the Governor I had an opportunity of observing some of the industries of the Sierra Leone population of some of the outlying towns. Aberdeen is the nearest town to the Cape point, the population of which is mainly occupied with fishing. On one occasion we saw the nets brought to land on the Atlantic coast. They had evidently been fixed at a short distance only from the shore, as the fish, of which enormous numbers were landed, did not exceed from 1 to 4 lbs. each in weight. Fish of many descriptions, including some of excellent quality, are very plentiful on the coast, and it only requires an increased demand to make this industry a very thriving one. Oysters of large size and excellent quality are found in abundance on some rocks near Cape point, and on the Bullom shore mangrove oysters are very plentiful; but though these latter are declared by many to be perfectly good, there is a considerable suspicion attaching to them in the eyes of the prudent.

A certain amount of cultivation is done in these outlying villages, principally of rice, cassava, and guinea-corn. Fruit is also grown, the most common kinds being bananas, oranges of a sweet but inferior flavour, papaws (a fruit in appearance like a melon, which grows on a tree), mangoes, and pines. Of these also it may be said, that if the quality is not all that it might be, it is probable that the number of those who possess a discriminating taste is too small to exercise any influence on the market. Throughout the interior the only fruit met with everywhere are bananas and papaws; hardly a village is to be found without these. Plantains are cultivated in the larger places only, and are too coarse to be eaten, except cooked as a vegetable.

The railway now being constructed from Freetown will, no doubt, have a great influence on the trade and prosperity of the colony. Considerable progress has been made with the line, in spite of the serious mortality amongst the engineers superintending the construction. There is something terribly dangerous about turning up the soil in West Africa; any work which involves doing this seems to set free malarial poison in its most deadly form. But in the face of these drawbacks the railway construction has made great progress, and it is hoped that in 1898 the first section, which ends at Songo Town, a distance from Freetown of about thirty miles, will be open for traffic. The line is to be continued in a south-easterly direction, towards the upper waters of the Sulima river, to tap a country which is rich in rubber, and comparatively well populated.

The effect of the railway construction is already being felt in Freetown; it has caused the most enterprising of its inhabitants to see that the time has come for modernizing their surroundings. The town is now ill lighted by oil lamps; some more suitable method is required. With a terminal station and railway works in progress, and with an important harbour, custom house, landing stage, coal wharves, and warehouses, the application of gas or electricity is a necessity.

A company has recently been formed to make soda water and ice for the West Coast generally, as well as for Sierra Leone in particular. Considering that the only good water to be found on the West Coast is at Freetown, and considering the demand for soda water and ice in a climate like that of the West Coast, it is a matter of surprise that this business has not been taken up earlier. The Company has secured the monopoly of a stream of excellent water, and should prove of much benefit to the Sierra Leone people.

Some attempts have been made by one of the leading men of Freetown to cultivate coffee in the neighbourhood of the place, and to export some of the fine timber growing on the hillsides, and I was informed that considerable profit had already been made from these sources.

On the 12th May the mail steamer "Benin" was signalled as arriving from the Gold Coast, and on the same afternoon I left the hospitable roof of the Governor, where I had spent a very pleasant four days, and returned by boat to Freetown, from which place our party embarked the next day, May 13th, on the "Benin," and left the same afternoon, arriving at Liverpool on the 29th May.

The French Commission left Wellia the day after our departure, and proceeded down the west bank to Konakri, where they embarked for France, arriving on the 21st of June.

The delimitation thus ended will, it may be hoped, put an end to the very unsatisfactory condition of affairs which has prevailed in the border country for years past. The exact frontier being unknown and the rights of each nation being undefined, the natives have been ignorant of their position with regard to Great Britain and France, and in some cases they have taken advantage of the opposing claims of both sides to further their own ends. In many places there are rival claimants to the position of Chieftainship of a district or Headmanship of a town. If the reigning party was of British sympathies, his rival was naturally French, and *vice versâ*; and the opposing parties did their part in keeping up friction, and in circulating reports of frontier violations, etc. Moreover, police patrols from British and French border stations traversed the doubtful zone, and occasionally came into collision with each other, both supposing themselves to be within their own territory. The boundary was only definitely settled by treaty in January 1895, and before this, more especially in the northern part of the Protectorate, it was impossible to say in any disputed case which party was in the right and which in the wrong. But even after the treaty had been signed, the position was little better, for frontier parties unprovided with instruments of precision could not lay down the law regarding a boundary dependent on a parallel of latitude or a line joining distant points in a country altogether unsurveyed.

Now, however, there can be no doubt about the frontier, and no one can cross it without knowing that he is doing so. In this country every one is confined to the roads, and every road is marked with a beacon at the place where it crosses the frontier.

Every village and town, therefore, near to the border knows on which territory it stands, and how its farm lands are divided. To make this doubly sure the border villages are all named in the *procès verbal*, and it is there stated on which side of the boundary they fall. The Chiefs and the Frontier Police have all had these matters explained to them, and if difficulties occur they can hardly be ascribed to ignorance except in very minor particulars.

As regards the general effect of the boundary, we found that the watershed line in the mountainous country made a very good natural frontier, and divided town from town in a very clear and unmistakable way. People belonging to the same district of Kuranko country are found living on both sides of the watershed in parts, but they are very well separated, and no difficulty should result from their being on one or the other side of the frontier. Further north, where the mountains disappear, the separation is not so clear, and the line occasionally cuts some farm land into one side, and other land belonging to the same town into the other side. In no case, however, on the watershed does the line cut through a village; every village is definitely on one side or the other.

In Samu, which is a country of many roads, the watershed boundary cuts the farms about, but the villages are all clearly on one or the other side.

Where the boundary is a parallel of latitude or a line joining two points, the division, as may naturally be expected, is not so satisfactory; but, fortunately, a great part of the country being uninhabited, no villages or farm lands are touched by the line, and no difficulties can occur.

It is to be hoped that, before many years are over, we may have every part of our African possessions and spheres, where they join those of other European powers, regularly demarcated and beaconed. The sooner this is done the better, as where the boundary is not a natural feature, difficulties of demarcation are increased if towns are built close to the border, or if farms or grazing lands are

L

taken up. The fixing of a frontier line on the ground, no doubt, is a necessary step to promote the development of a country, and until it is carried out little can be done where boundaries are undefined.

# CHAPTER VII

## THE PEOPLE OF THE SIERRA LEONE PROTECTORATE

THE remarks made here on the people of the Protectorate with whom I came in contact during the expedition described in this work must not be taken as having the same value as those of an observer who has spent years in the country, and has had special opportunities of studying the native character. To lay down the law after an experience of not more than six months of a country, and to generalize from the small number of natives with whom one is brought into contact in a short time, are, I am well aware, very likely to lead one from mistaken premises to wrong conclusions. I can only speak of the native character as it showed itself to me, and reproduce the impressions fixed on my mind.

The people with whom I came in contact in greater or less numbers are the Sierra Leonis, the Timmeni, the Mendi, the Limba, the Kuranko, and the Susu. All these people speak different languages, although there is a considerable similarity between some of them, and all the languages are of Arabic origin, excepting, of course, the pigeon-English spoken by the Sierra Leonis.

Of the Sierra Leonis I have spoken already. They possess a civilization of their own; some of them indeed, as I have remarked before, are highly educated and accomplished. The children are trained and educated under the direction of the Church Missionary Society, and the whole population is nominally Christian. Every village has its church, generally a bare white-washed building, and the people are very regular in their attendance at the services. Any one who has been inside one of their churches, and has heard the crowded congregation singing in every conceivable key, not as English people sing, but each member devoting his or her full lung power to the work, will not readily forget the effect.

The Sierra Leonis are affable to a fault. As you meet them in the street, you are greeted with a broad grin, and a "Good morning, sah." They are absolutely free from the reserve of northern races, and are only too anxious to open their souls to any passer-by. Their cheerfulness, too, is beyond all praise, and rises superior to the enervating effect of the climate. Indeed the more nearly the conditions which depress the Europeans are attained in their highest degree, the more cheerful and the more affable does the Sierra Leone become. Their faults are those common to all natives of the West Coast, and probably are the result in some cases of a low order of civilization, and in others of a want of the sense of responsibility. The most striking are untruthfulness and dishonesty, and, especially in the lower classes, these faults are common. At the same time, they are not universal, and amongst the natives with whom

I was brought in contact were some whose character in these matters was beyond reproach. The Sierra Leonis are distinctly not a warlike people. Many of them are men of fine physique, but fighting is not their strong point, and no one can fail to observe in them the absence of those qualities which go to make a nation of warriors. Though the physique of the men is fine, they are not, as a rule, capable of sustaining great hardships, and constitutionally, I imagine, they are not as strong as their appearance suggests. They are specially subject to chest diseases; indeed, all the natives of the West Coast seem to suffer from bronchitis and other kindred ailments in chronic form.

Of the Timmeni people we saw very little, and amongst our followers we had only one or two representatives of that race, so I am not in a position to give any account of their special characteristics. This applies also to the Limba, of whom we only came in contact with a small body. The Limba appear, however, so far as my observation extended, to be in advance of other tribes in comparative civilization. A great many of the traders who travel into the interior are Limba, Mohammedans of a superior kind. As a race the Limba appear also to be more self-reliant and more warlike than other West Africans.

The Mendi form the bulk of the population which affords recruits for expeditions. The main body of our carriers were Mendi boys. They come from the Sherboro country, situated in the southern part of Sierra Leone. They are all pagans, intensely ignorant and superstitious, and very low in the scale of civilization. They are strong, powerful men, hard workers, willing, and capable of severe exertion under great privations. Their good qualities are most apparent when their circumstances are most adverse; prosperity only brings out their vices. When half starved they will work without complaint till they drop, and they have no notion of giving in. I should be loth to recommend that a Mendi boy should be flogged daily and half starved; yet I cannot doubt, from my experience of him, that such a treatment would bring out the best side of his nature and keep down his vices.

At the same time, though valuable and courageous workers, the Mendi are collectively of no value for fighting purposes, nor are they to be dreaded as enemies. There is amongst them no discipline, cohesion, or binding motive to give them the power of carrying out a common purpose. They have the greatest dread of white men, and are ready to obey them like slaves do their masters.

All the other races of West Africa treat the Mendi with scorn and abuse. It is the greatest insult possible to call a Susu a "Mendi boy," and I sometimes found this term a useful way of reproving the Susu servant and hammock-boys. Even the Kuranko, timid as they are, never failed to attack the Mendi boys when circumstances were sufficiently favourable to them. At Kruto, one of our carriers was seriously assaulted by the people. I endeavoured to fathom the reason of the hostility of the Kuranko, supposing that the Mendi must have committed some offence. The

Chief at first made one excuse after another, but, on being pressed, said at last that the truth was the carrier was a Mendi, and that when his people found a Mendi alone, they could not help attacking him; it was in their blood.

The Mendi appear to be above the weakness of personal vanity; they take no pains to adorn themselves. Their clothing is of the lightest order, and generally in a fragmentary condition.

The extraordinary superstitiousness of this people has recently been practically demonstrated by what are called the leopard murders in the Imperri district. These murders, of which many cases have been reported, are committed by men dressed up in leopard skins, and armed with a sharp-pointed knife attached by a ring to each wrist. The wearer of the leopard skin watches in the bush any unwary person who passes near him, and, coming behind his victim, he brings his two knives together in the unsuspecting man's throat. The object of these murders is to obtain parts of the murdered man's body, which are supposed to confer great advantages on the murderer.

Of the Kuranko I have spoken before, and need only say here that, though superstitious and ignorant, and though they have not been brought into contact with the white people and their civilization, as have the Mendi, they are yet somewhat in advance of the latter. Perhaps the Mohammedan element, of which there is a sprinkling in Kuranko country, has something to do with their superiority.

The Susu, who occupy the country along the Great Skarsies river, and the northern boundary of the Protectorate, are a very different people from either Kuranko or Mendi. They are to be found generally as hammock-boys and servants, and in superior positions. They are Mohammedans, and, as such, greatly in advance of the pagans and fetish worshippers. They are intelligent, self-reliant, and brave, often of great strength and activity, and able to undergo great fatigues.

Morally, they are enormously superior to the Mendi, whom they regard with great contempt. They are not, however, gifted with the dumb endurance of the Mendi, and if they suffer, it is not in silence. They are generally vain and very fond of show; they will travel through the bush with hardly a rag on, but when they enter a town will dress themselves in flowing robes and bright colours. Some of our boys seemed to buy a different change of apparel at every place of importance they entered.

The Susu generally are excellent marchers and mountaineers. They were of great service in helping us to climb rocks, gorges, and deep places, and to get over swamps and rivers. I was always accompanied by a powerful Susu hammock-boy, who brought me sucessfully through every difficulty. These boys are very attentive and very faithful, and make good servants and attendants, and are often of great use in dealing with the natives of villages passed through when anything is required.

As the Susu are more advanced than the Kuranko and Mendi, so their requirements are higher. They expect better feeding and better treatment, and they are more ready to complain than the others when they have to put up with hard work and starvation diet. They are not by any means as submissive as the Mendi, and are apt to resent the discipline imposed on them in camp and on the march. Like the Limba, they are much more warlike than the Kuranko and Mendi, and might be made into good soldiers.

But, although the natives of the Protectorate differ in degree as regards their fighting capacities, none of the people are, in any but a comparative sense, warlike, nor is it likely that they will ever be difficult to keep under control. Favoured by local circumstances, such as, for instance, a position like Kurubundo, a native Chief may give trouble for a few weeks, but no more serious difficulty is to be anticipated. The country is no doubt well suited for those who seek to resist authority, but the people possess neither initiative,

# PEOPLE OF SIERRA LEONE 173

cohesion, nor strength of purpose sufficient to give serious trouble.

The real fighting races of this part of West Africa hail from the French side of the border. The men we saw with caravans of trade from the Middle Niger, or travelling with their slaves to Freetown, are splendidly built, of great stature, and with the bearing, dignity, and manner of gentlemen. It is easy to see that the people of which these men are representatives must be independent, patriotic, and imbued with strong religious feelings. To subdue such a race must be a work of great difficulty, requiring much judgment, but when the task has been done, a grand field for recruiting soldiers and officials will be opened up.

Again, the Senegalese and the people of Futa Jallon are fine, hardy fellows, fighting men by birth, and, under the leading of white officers, no better troops can be found. Their value has been proved in the many campaigns which the French have waged against the Sofas, and in their expedition against Dahome. They are splendid marchers, full of self-reliance, and can be trusted alone to carry out any task confided to them.

The strong point common to all the natives of the British Protectorate is their light-heartedness. No one who has not met these West Africans knows what laughing means. Nor is there any limit to the occasions on which they indulge in merriment. They laugh when most men are inclined to take a very opposite course. Their very sins are productive of merriment. When they are convicted of theft they laugh, when caught in a lie they roar, and if, during the time that they are expiating their crimes, their merriment ceases, I am convinced that this is rather from motives of policy than because they do not thoroughly appreciate the humour of the situation. Indeed the highest form of amusement possible for a native is to see his brother or dearest friend undergoing the penalty of the law. In dealing with these people one is at first led to plume oneself with the belief that there is something peculiarly humorous about one's expressions and

# PEOPLE OF SIERRA LEONE 175

remarks, but when one hears the remarks of a friend, which strike one as singularly commonplace, greeted with the same roars of laughter, this flattering imagination is speedily dissipated. In civilized lands few men can pose as humorists with success; in West Africa, do what he will, no one can escape from having this honour thrust upon him.

It is impossible to give any even very rough estimate of the population of the Protectorate. About certain parts the villages are numerous and close together. This is especially the case along the Great Skarsies, south of Kukuna. The villages here are not only very numerous, but of a good size. The largest towns we saw contained not more than a hundred huts, which would place the population at not more than 1000 souls, as nearly as I can judge. But there were few towns as big as this; Kambia and Kukuna alone, I should say, had as many as a hundred huts. In the second rank, with between fifty and a hundred huts, come Kiridugu, Bumban, Port Lokko, Kruto, Berea Futambu, Saionia, and

Berekuri. Kuranko country, generally, is sparsely populated, but it is impossible to say how many of the people are still hiding in the bush, and may return to towns when they realize that they are under protection. But under any circumstances the population cannot be large, and it will need some years of settled government before cultivation can cover more than a very small percentage of the area of the country.

In the southern part of the Protectorate the population is greater than in the north, and there are many fair-sized towns extending right up to the Liberian frontier. From a very rough estimate, based partly upon observation and partly upon hearsay, I should say that the total number of natives in the Protectorate does not exceed 500,000, but it must be understood that no sufficient data are forthcoming to give any real value to these figures. The country has not yet been by any means thoroughly explored, and it is possible that many towns may be found whose existence is at present unknown to the civilized world.

The people of these countries are remarkably amenable to the native administration in force. The government is of the patriarchal order: a country is ruled by a Chief, under whom are sub-chiefs, who again exercise authority over the head-men of villages. The Chief appears to be obeyed without hesitation, although the only executive he possesses consists of the people themselves. As far as I could learn crimes against property and person are rare; at any rate, any action of the executive is uncommon. Political intrigue and faction are not unknown, especially with regard to the position of Chief of a district, or to the possession of certain lands by one tribe or another, but I saw or heard very little of the crimes of the individual. The Chiefs told me that for stealing or violence they order the offender's hand to be cut off, but they said that this punishment was in practice very rarely resorted to, and I never met with an instance of a man who had been so treated. At Bumban, indeed, the Chief with his own hands flogged one of his people, and had him marched through the town in chains, the nominal charge being that he had stolen something from our people; but I believe this was done mainly as a sort of compliment to the British Commission, and, perhaps, also to exemplify how sternly the law was administered in his dominions. But, except in this case, I never heard of the law being put in motion against any native, and I am bound to believe that the people are, as a rule, a law-abiding race. I do not desire to imply that thefts are unknown with them; far from it; but I conclude that the interchange of property rarely takes such unnatural proportions as to call for the interposition of the law, and I quite believe that crimes of individual violence are very rare.

All property belongs to the Chief, who distributes it as he pleases. Our presents were always made to the Chief, but he was either generous or polite enough to give his followers a fair share of what he received.

The Protectorate is, I believe, being administered by the native law as it stands, all barbarous punishments and methods being, of course, excluded. I have no doubt that little difficulty will be experienced in ruling the country in this way, and that the people will prove amenable to the management of the white man so long as their customs and mode of life are not seriously interfered with.

The West African natives are not long lived. They are not, indeed, subject to the diseases which are specially fatal to Europeans dwelling in their country, and, as regards malaria, their constitutions appear to have become inoculated with the germs of the poison, and they enjoy immunity more or less complete from fevers. But they suffer from their own ailments, of which chest diseases and smallpox are the chief. For working purposes a man over thirty-five is of very little value, and a man of forty is regarded as an old man. Our oldest carrier was about forty, and he, though relieved from carrying a load, broke down at Tembi Kunda, and died of bronchitis. One rarely meets a man of the apparent age of sixty in the interior. It is, of course, not possible to ascertain exact ages; one can only judge from appearances, but old men are certainly not very plentiful.

As regards the female sex, the views prevalent in Europe and America seem to have made little way in West Africa; the woman is little better than a slave and a beast of burden. The hard work falls mainly on the women; the privileges are confined to the male sex. The women cultivate the fields, card and spin cotton, beat the husk rice, and prepare the food. The men work also in the fields, cut roads, and build huts, so that all the heavy manual labour is not, as in some parts of Africa, laid upon the women. In all ceremonials, processions, palavers, and dances, the men only take part, but occasionally the women act as a sort of chorus to applaud the dancing of a Chief.

Polygamy is prevalent everywhere in the interior, but it is the privilege of the select few. The rank and file of a West African village have rarely more than one wife, whilst the Chief, according to his status, numbers his wives and female slaves by tens or even hundreds. I understand that many of the Chiefs consider the entire womankind of their country to be their property, and they tell off those whom they do not consider good enough to keep themselves to their relatives, friends, and subjects.

We were shown in Kuranko country whips with thongs of strips of leather, which we were informed were used for beating the women. On being told that in our country no one ever struck a woman, great astonishment was expressed, and we were asked how we got our chop (food) without resorting to the whip. I am bound to say, however, that although we spent many hours, day after day, in native villages, and had daily opportunities for observing the native ways, no single instance of harshness towards a woman came under our notice.

In certain parts of the interior, especially in the coast region, the custom of *bundi*, or the performance of a degrading operation on young girls approaching the age of puberty, is carried out with great ceremony. The girls are kept in a separate house and distinguished by a special dress for a month before the date, and the day is observed with dancing and festivities.

DANCE OF A BUNDI PRIEST ON OCCASION OF CEREMONY

# CHAPTER VIII

## THE DEVELOPMENT OF THE INTERIOR, AND THE INFLUENCE UPON IT OF THE HEALTH QUESTION

IN the last chapter on several occasions I have made use of the word "Protectorate." It should have been mentioned earlier that the territory lying within the Anglo-French boundary, as recently demarcated, and the Anglo-Liberian boundary, and outside of the colony of Sierra Leone proper, which till 1896 was merely a British sphere of influence, was last year declared a Protectorate. Deputy-Commissioners have been appointed to look after the administration of this country, one to each Frontier Police district, and the number of white men permanently quartered in the interior is thus doubled.

It has become a matter of considerable importance to consider what is to be done with regard to developing this country, containing, as it does, from 15,000 to 20,000 square miles of territory. The exact area of the British Protectorate cannot be ascertained till the course of the Mano river has been mapped. From the data now in our possession I make it out to be something over 18,000 square miles. That a serious effort must be made to win this large extent of ground to commerce and to civilization is, I think, a postulate which no one will be inclined to question. The many valuable lives which have been sacrificed in opening up the country are all pledges of our intention to complete the task, pledges which still remain to be redeemed. It is a very remarkable thing that, though this land lies so near to our shores, not a penny has been spent in developing it. The interior trade has, indeed, been sought for, and promoted, but the country of the Protectorate is to-day untouched. On its fifteen or twenty thousand square miles nothing is produced but the little the natives require for their daily wants, and what nature, unaided, puts forth. What the ground is capable of, experience alone can decide. The soil is undoubtedly fertile, water is abundant everywhere, and cultivation can be carried on without artificial irrigation. The rice grown in the country is of the best quality as regards flavour and size, though it is said that the English merchants will not touch it on account of a slight reddish tinge it has after being cleaned. Tobacco of an inferior quality is grown in abundance, but I believe there is no reason why a leaf of the best quality should not be just as easily cultivated. Coffee of a marketable kind is now produced in the colony of Sierra Leone and in Liberia, and the interior should be able at least to do what the coast can do. Many parts of the hilly country are well suited for coffee growing. Fruit and vegetables of every species suited to tropical climates grow readily in Freetown, and could undoubtedly be produced anywhere in the interior. But the country included in the Protectorate now supplies to the markets of Europe nothing but palm oil, palm kernels, ground nuts, kola nuts, and rubber. The palm oil and kernels are obtained mainly from the Sherboro country, the rubber and kola from the interior, especially the south-eastern part. Kola nuts grow everywhere in the highlands and are very valuable. A considerable trade in this product is carried on with the French Sudan. Rubber is found in all the valleys along the eastern and northern boundaries, as well as in the south-eastern districts, where it is still more abundant. It is obtained either from the rubber tree, or from the rubber vine, a creeper which twines round the stems of the large trees. But in Kuranko country nothing is understood concerning the value of rubber, and, as I was often told by the Chief, the people have never been taught how to extract it from the tree. In the Sulima country I am told that the natives are destroying the trees in order to extract the rubber. It comes forth in the form of a white gum wherever an incision is made, and some knowledge is necessary to make the incision in such a way as not to injure the tree or creeper. The destruction of the trees is a serious matter for the prospects of the country. Well-instructed natives would, no doubt, make considerable profits if they were taught how the maximum of rubber might be secured without injury to the plants, and it is to be hoped that steps may be taken to protect this very important industry.

But granting the productive power of the country, and the value of what it can supply for export, the cost of carriage to the coast is so great as to eat up all profits which the producer can make by the sale of his goods. Bulky articles can, indeed, hardly be transported at all. Roughly speaking, the cost of carriage at Sierra Leone prices would add $2\frac{1}{2}$d. per lb. for every 100 miles to the price at which an article must be disposed of to secure a profit. This is entirely due to the carrier system in force in West Africa. It cannot be doubted that this system can never be applied with success to matters of commerce where a civilized government exists; it is possible only where slavery is in force. The caravans from the Middle Niger which come to Freetown in the dry season consist of gangs of slaves bearing loads, with their masters. But this system is impossible for British subjects, and the whole question of the development of the country is in the first place a matter of the opening up of communications, and the substitution of some more profitable means of transport for the native carrier. The railway line now being constructed to Songo Town, and eventually to reach the upper Sulima river country, will form the main trunk line for the trade of the most productive part of the Protectorate, but it will tap but a small part of the country, and much more is required. Good roads, wide enough for wheel traffic, with arrangements for crossing the unfordable rivers, are the first requirement. In the northern half of the Protectorate roads are required (1) from Kambia and Kukuna to Saionia, Yana, and Dumbaia, and to the plateaux formed by the spurs north of the last-named place, as well

# THE HEALTH QUESTION 189

as to the French frontier at Ula; (2) from Port Lokko to Bumban and Falaba, and thence to Simitia, to Kalieri, to Berea Futambu and Heremakono, and to Berea Timbako and Songoia Tintarba; (3) from Port Lokko or Rokell to Kruto, and thence to Kurubundo, Bali, and Samaindu. As to the roads required in the southern part of the Protectorate, it is impossible to speak without a knowledge of the country, but it seems probable that at least two main roads terminating at Senahu and Sulima, and converging towards Kaure Lahun, are necessary.

No great difficulty is to be faced in the construction of these roads. It would be sufficient in the coast region to indicate the direction, and in the mountainous country to mark out the lines, to be followed; the local Chiefs would naturally be responsible for clearing and keeping clear the track to the required width, and once it began to be used, the wheels would keep down the vegetation. The swamps are a difficulty, but elephant grass and wood are so plentiful everywhere, that it would be possible without much labour to corduroy them. An arrangement, such as the pontoon in use in South Africa, would serve to ferry carts across the larger rivers, and could be worked by means of the creepers which are so abundant on the river banks.

It has been supposed that cattle and horses cannot exist in the interior. Whatever may be the case in Freetown itself and the immediate neighbourhood, it is certainly not so up country. That cattle and horses are not numerous in Kuranko country is due entirely to the poverty of the people and to the Sofa raids. What animals are to be found are in a flourishing condition, and the Chiefs all told me they thrive well. In the hill country of Tamisso, the large herds of cattle we saw were all in the best possible state. As regards transport animals, the experience furnished by the French riding mules is of great value. These animals, four in number, were obtained from the transport company at Dakar; they accompanied the expedition

# THE HEALTH QUESTION

everywhere, and were ridden daily through every description of country. They swam the unfordable rivers; crossed the worst swamps with the aid of bundles of elephant grass thrown down on the spongy ground; climbed every mountain with the footmen, and were never defeated. They were fed with grain (rice or guinea-corn), when grain was available, and when not available they grazed the herbage to be found. They were never sick, and at the end of the work were all in the best condition. The advantages of mules, as opposed to hammocks, are very great, especially when working off the main roads; a hammock cannot be used except on a road which has been cleared of bush; if it is attempted, the occupant experiences many pleasing surprises by finding himself projected, in sitting attitude, with great violence against a stump of a tree, or a strong shrub. After a few such surprises only the most reckless will attempt to ride in the West African carriage again, except on the best of roads. The mule, on the other hand, goes everywhere, and rarely makes a mistake. Again, the five or six hammock-boys allowed to each hammock are a serious strain on commissariat resources and a great expense; the mule requires but one attendant, and where there are a number of mules, one attendant between two or three is enough.

The French have very justly a great faith in mules; they have used them in all their West African possessions, and in the Dahome campaign they found them very valuable. It is strange that no attempt has been made in British colonies to use even pack, transport, or riding mules. Considering the costliness of carriers, the difficulty of feeding them and of maintaining discipline amongst them, the advantages of the substitution of mules would be very great.

There is no tsetse fly in any part of the country our expedition passed through, and I think it is very unlikely that any conditions exist unfavourable to the life of horse or mule anywhere within the Protectorate, except perhaps near the coast in the low country.

The Sofas brought large numbers of horses into the northern and eastern parts of the country when they invaded it, and for a long time had a considerable establishment at and about Heremakono. They have for years marched, countermarched, and fought in the parts of the Western Sudan which join the Sierra Leone Protectorate, and have always been accompanied by a large proportion of mounted men.

As far as the interior trade goes, the difficulty of revolutionizing the system of transport lies herein, that the trade is entirely in the hands of the natives. The British trader has nothing to do with it; he buys at the coast and sells at the coast, and there his interest ceases. Small native traders from places within the Protectorate occasionally take up portable articles into the interior, with which they buy rubber, kola, and gold, but of the British trade goods sold in the year the principal part is handed across the counter in the factories at Freetown and other coast towns to pay for the articles of export brought down from the interior. These articles are carried after a system more or less directly allied to slavery, and to abolish such a system on economical grounds is no easy task. But the merchant has much to gain by bringing his wares to the consumer, or as near to him as he can conveniently get. He is able then not only to deal directly with the consumer, but also to watch over the production of the articles of export with which his goods are paid for. What is required, in short, is the establishment in the interior of stations and factories, where the natives under the supervision of experts can cultivate coffee, tobacco, indigo, kola, grain, rubber trees, and everything which can be grown at a profit, and where at the same time British trade goods can be sold.

But the question then arises, Can the European exist in the interior of West Africa, or can life there be rendered endurable both as regards the prospect of health and the surroundings? Upon the answer to this question the development of our West African possessions entirely depends. It is from beginning to end a matter of health. Indeed, everything connected with the West Coast must be considered first and foremost from the health point of view. The climate has an evil reputation, which those most interested in the development of the country cannot gainsay, and I certainly should be the last to recommend Sierra Leone as the most suitable place for a young man to settle in. Still, the devil is not so black as he is painted, and the climate of Sierra Leone is not responsible for all the fatalities which have been attributed to it. As regards the interior, I desire to speak with caution. The casual visitor has no right to constitute himself a judge of a country which he has not seen at all seasons and under all circumstances, and the layman has no right to lay down the law on matters which lie within the province of the medical expert. I confine myself, therefore, to saying that outside of the coast region, *i.e.* at an elevation of from 1500 to 3000 feet above sea level, the air is perceptibly much fresher, the capacity for work is undoubtedly greater, and the night temperature, as recorded by the thermometer, is, in the dry season at least, much lower than in the low country. It is an undisputable fact that the Frontier Police officers quartered in the interior have suffered greatly from fever, and that the mortality amongst them has been exceptionally great. But, on the other hand, it must be borne in mind that these officers have lived beyond the reach of the comforts and necessaries which, as every dweller on the West Coast admits, are essential to the maintenance of health. In such a climate, to rough it on what the country affords is to court fever. Every man should live well, at any rate in the sense that his menu should include first-class groceries and articles of a high food value; but this is impossible to any one dependent on carrier transport. Where good communications exist, the difficulty passes away. But the Frontier Police officers in the interior have hitherto been quartered at places which, with one exception, that of Falaba, may be said to belong to the coast region, and not to the high lands. At Falaba the officers have suffered very little from fever, and I learned from one, who left Falaba before our expedition got to Tembi Kunda, that during fifteen months' stay at that place he had never once suffered from fever. We learned also from the French officers that their Sudan stations, which join our frontier posts, have been very unhealthy for some years, but that by adopting sanitary measures, and by making the places as comfortable as circumstances admitted, the rate of invaliding has been greatly reduced, and that the sickness recently has been trifling.

There can be no doubt that in making an European settlement care should be taken to adopt the strictest sanitary precautions, and particularly to protect from contamination the water supply. The natives themselves are very careless on this matter, and on many occasions we found them using for drinking purposes water which had already done duty for flushing sewage. Again, it is very necessary that the ground should be trenched in making a station, both for building purposes, and also for the cultivation of vegetables; but in doing this care must be taken, for to turn up the ground has always been found to be an unfailing cause of fever.

There are several places in the northern half of the Protectorate where posts might be established for Europeans. The high ground of the watershed on the eastern frontier is well suited to such a purpose, as is also the country between Kruto and Falaba. Further west the plateaux above Dumbaia would make a place, if difficult to reach, at any rate very pleasant to live in, and here a cattle industry might be carried on with profit.

In any of the higher parts of the country posts may be established with little difficulty. Whatever may be the disadvantages of the Sierra Leone Protectorate, one is always certain of finding water and fuel within easy distance of any place selected as a station. The water is not always of the best quality, although I believe the water in this part is, generally speaking, better than in the other

British Colonies and Dependencies of West Africa; but water of fairly good quality can generally be met with near all stations, and it would be a very easy matter to arrange stations in good positions near a good water supply and at the same time within easy reach of the main trade routes. In order that a station should have the greatest prospect of being healthy for Europeans it should have a height above sea level of not less than 1500 feet, and it should be on the highest ground in the neighbourhood, which should be, as far as possible, open and free from swamp. The worst swamps are found in the low ground of the coast region, but bad swamps are also met with in country of a relative height of 1500 feet. Above this level swamp is found in the valleys, but not of so deep and foul a kind as in the lower countries.

There are plenty of places within the Protectorate which satisfy all these conditions, and granted that good communication is made from the places selected to the coast, so that European supplies can be sent up cheaply, I am convinced that these stations will be found healthier than those on the coast, and much pleasanter to live in. Indeed, if any towns could once be established in the best parts of the interior, I believe that, after they had undergone a period of probation of a year or two, the climate of West Africa would obtain a better reputation. One of the worst features of Freetown is the complete absence of any form of occupation or recreation for the European population during their spare time. In the interior they would at least find some interesting sport, and they would have energy for some of the recreations which the climate of the coast excludes.

One of the most necessary steps to the development of the country is the encouragement of the native population to settle in their own countries, and to devote themselves to cultivating the soil. Hitherto the people of the eastern frontier have been driven to seek shelter in the bush in various parts of the country, whilst their lands have gone out of cultivation, and their towns have been

# THE HEALTH QUESTION

destroyed; and the peoples of other parts have been drawn away from their villages to the coast to seek work as carriers, servants, and hammock-boys. A large trade has always been done in Freetown in organizing carrier transport, and the work has a singular attraction for the native, not because he receives more than when paid by the day in Freetown, but because, not being paid till the expedition with which he serves returns to the coast, he comes in for an accumulation which represents a small fortune to him. Carriers have been collected at Freetown for the various wars on the West Coast in the Gambia, Gold Coast, Lagos, and Niger territories, and large numbers have been seduced by promises of high pay to go and serve in the Congo Free State as labourers on the railway or as soldiers. The country has to some extent suffered depopulation by the large drafts enlisted for the Congo Free State, and this matter has become so serious that the Governor of Sierra Leone has now put a stop to it. If the carrier transport system is to meet with the death which it certainly deserves, and is to be succeeded by some more modern and less expensive method, the large floating population of Freetown will have to seek for work in some other direction, and it may be hoped they will return to their villages and increase the production of the country.

The future of the country is, I imagine, entirely dependent on the cultivation of the products of the soil. Of mineral wealth, I believe, there is little indication. The geological formation, as far as we could trace it, appears to vary little throughout the country. What exposed rock surfaces we saw were of volcanic origin, and consisted of granite, and quartzose rock or laterite, except only in the country of the Tamisso hills, which are composed of schistose stratified rock. It may be that in the future prospectors will discover something of value hidden beneath the surface of the ground, but, according to our present information, the Sierra Leone interior does not possess the hidden wealth which is believed to exist in the Gold Coast colony.

# THE HEALTH QUESTION

To recapitulate: the main steps to be taken in developing the country are to open up a regular system of communication for wheel transport, and to establish posts on the high ground of the interior. Traders might be induced to settle in the interior, representing companies with concessions to work certain districts, and they could promote the cultivation of such products as might be grown most profitably. The natives should be encouraged to settle in their own countries and to cultivate the soil.

As an additional reason for settling in the interior, it should be mentioned that the coast region is subject to very fatal forms of fevers, at intervals of two or three years, which carry off many lives. During the present year, 1897, Sierra Leone has suffered severely. Some valuable lives have been lost; amongst others Dr. Paris, the native surgeon who accompanied our expedition, the Governor's aide-de-camp, and the Chief Justice have fallen victims to the prevailing unhealthiness. I imagine that the virulent form of fever, which does such havoc at intervals at Sierra Leone and on the coast, would not be found in the most favourably situated positions in the interior, and that selected stations would thus escape the serious mortality which prevails on the coast in unhealthy seasons. I speak in this matter entirely without book, but so far as general information goes, the bad type of fever is limited to the coast region in epidemic form.

# CHAPTER IX

## THE GEOGRAPHY AND TOPOGRAPHY OF THE SIERRA LEONE PROTECTORATE

THE geography of the country lying behind the coast line of Sierra Leone has been exceedingly difficult to evolve. It has taken many years of exploration to arrive at the knowledge we now possess, and many valuable lives have been sacrificed in contributing to the work. Even now our knowledge of the country included within the new Protectorate is far from complete, and a wide field is still open for explorers to fill up the many gaps which exist. Yet this very country has been scored by the routes of travellers, soldiers, and explorers, and during the present century a perfect army of Europeans has marched through it at different times and in different directions, many of whom bear names that are famous in the history of African exploration.

It has been traversed first by Major Gordon Laing, who in 1822 passed near to the sources of the Niger, obtaining a distant view of the Loma Mountain, which was believed to overlook the head waters of the river. Different parts of the interior were visited in 1827 by R. Caillié, in 1842 by W. C. Thompson, in 1851 by H. Hecquard, in 1860 by Lambert, in 1863 by Benjamin Anderson, and in 1869 and 1873 by Winwood Reade. In 1872 Dr. Blyden travelled from the coast by Bafodeya to Falaba, and in 1879 Zweifel and Moustier reached the Niger sources from Falaba, and gave to the world a description of them, placing the Tembi source in 8° 36′ N. latitude and 12° 53′ W. longitude (Paris), or thirty-one geographical miles north and fourteen miles east of the position as fixed by our Commission, and the sources of the Faliko in 8° 45′ N. latitude and 12° 45′ W. longitude (Paris), or $25\frac{2}{3}$ geographical miles north of the position as fixed by the French Commissioners.

# GEOGRAPHY AND TOPOGRAPHY

In 1882 Herr Ernst Vohsen, afterwards Administrator of German East Africa, and now, as the head of the famous Berlin firm of Dietrich Reimer & Co., one of the most consistent supporters of geographical exploration, visited Timmeni country, accompanied by Dr. W. Hume Hart and E. Keller. And amongst the more recent explorers are Major Festing, who visited Samory's country, and afterwards sacrificed his life to the effects of the climate; Lieut. Dumbleton, R.E., who, with Mr. Gouldsbury, marched from the Gambia to Sierra Leone; Mr. Garrett, who also fell a victim to the climate after rendering valuable services to geography; Major Kenney, R.E., who explored the northern frontier as far as Farana on the Niger in 1891; Colonel Ellis' expedition, which traversed the south-east part of the Protectorate in 1893-94, with the object of driving out the Sofas; and the present Governor, Sir F. Cardew, who has made systematic explorations of the interior every dry season since he first came out, and has secured some valuable information, especially in 1895, when accompanied by Captain Compton, R.N., and in 1896 when Major Grant, R.E., was his assistant.

For years the drainage system, that infallible guide to the topography of a country, was altogether misunderstood, and the credit of first clearing up the course of the Melakore and the Great and Small Skarsies rivers belongs to Mr. Garrett, who contributed, before his untimely death, a great deal of most valuable information on the geography and topography of the interior, proving how a painstaking, self-instructed colonial official can utilize to the greatest advantage the opportunities which are put in his way, when his official duties lead him to unknown parts of the country. But the drainage system of the east and south part of the Protectorate still remains to be defined by future explorers, and the courses of the Seli, Bagwe, Bafi, Bafin, Ngeyi, Mantili, Mano, Kittam, Sulima, and many other large rivers, are still very vaguely known and probably very incorrectly described by cartographers.

The country, as this narrative has explained, is one particularly difficult to explore, from its dense covering of bush, from the want of conspicuous and easily recognizable landmarks, and from the difficulty of seeing long distances through the hazy, moist atmosphere; and it is little to be wondered at that individual travellers, making routes through the interior, without accurate instruments, and having no fixed points to close on, should have led cartographers from one mistake to another. But little by little information of a more or less exact description has been collected, till we are at last in possession of so many points fixed with such reasonable claims to accuracy that almost any route made in the future can be referred to one or more of them. From time to time different observers have contributed a number of latitudes, and in some cases many observations at different times and by different hands have been made of the same place. Many longitudes depending upon chronometer ratings have also been observed, and, as naturally might be expected, widely divergent results have been worked out from the observations of different explorers for the same position. Still, in some cases, so many observations have been taken, that, eliminating the most discordant results, the mean should give a very fair value for the longitude. Thus we have places like Kambia, Bumban, Kukuna, Bafodeya, Falaba, and Wellia, fixed with considerable accuracy as regards latitude, and within a probable error of two or three miles in longitude. In addition to these places many towns have been fixed in latitude, and single observations for time have been made at them. Very valuable results were obtained by Major Kenney, C.M.G., in 1891, who worked from the mouth of the Great Skarsies to Wellia and thence to Falaba and Sulimania, observing the latitude and times. The longitudes obtained on this occasion require only the confirmation of later observers.

So much was known before the commencement of the work described in this book, and on the data already obtained our work was in a great part based. In marching from Port

# GEOGRAPHY AND TOPOGRAPHY

Lokko to Bumban no route traverse was made, but the daily distance marched was checked by using a perambulator, and observations for latitude were made at every halt. The distances of each day's march, as recorded, are given in the itinerary. The perambulator, I may remark, is an instrument whose value cannot be exaggerated for work in a difficult country. Whatever the ground was like, whether rocky or bush covered, the perambulator always worked well, and the distances recorded were fully confirmed by the results obtained by astronomical observations. We had, indeed, some little difficulty to contend with at first. The carrier who was told off to wheel the perambulator had been brought up, like every West African, in the belief that his head was given to him to serve the purpose of a saddle on which to rest the 50 or 60 lbs. which it was his trade to carry daily, and that to lend himself to any other form of transport was to fly in the face of nature. Therefore, whenever he escaped from observation, he would pick up the wheel and carry it on his head. But we succeeded in curing him of this inherited prejudice before long, and in convincing him that he was most valuable when his head was used for no purpose save as an ornament. The perambulator survived the roughest roads and the most difficult trackless country. It was used for our route traverse from Port Lokko to Tembi Kunda; it then rested while we were working from trigonometrical points, till we reached the difficult country at the northern end of the watershed boundary. We used it to run a traverse from Salamaia to Songoia Tintarba, and to work from thence to Kalieri, to traverse all the roads about Kalieri, and to take us to the 10th parallel. Along the 10th parallel it was used to the Kaba river, and thence to the Kita-Lolo junction, and it finally broke down within a day's march of this point. From thence onward distances were paced to Kukuna, every member of the British mission recording his pacing, and a mean of results being adopted. The pedometer we found useless; it recorded fairly well on a road, but

# GEOGRAPHY AND TOPOGRAPHY 213

in crossing country was altogether untrustworthy.

The map attached to this work has been constructed in the following way: Port Lokko has been placed in the position assigned to it in previous maps, which is based on Admiralty charts. Bumban has been fixed in the latitude obtained by the British Commission, 9° 7′ 15″ (previous observations giving it as 9° 7′ 19″, 9° 7′ 13″, 9° 7′ 7″, 9° 7′ 13″), and in longitude 11° 55′ 32″, the mean of two observations taken by Mr. Garrett and Captain Compton, our meridian distance giving it as 11° 56′ 8″. The places between Port Lokko and Bumban have been adjusted by the observations for latitude and the perambulator distances between the two terminal points as fixed above.

From Bumban a route traverse was made by the British Commission to the Niger sources. This was divided into two stages, the first of which closed at Kruto. The Governor, who explored the country from the Niger sources southwards, was accompanied by Major Grant, R.E., an observer of the highest qualifications, who had surveyed the Anglo-Portuguese frontier in South-East Africa with the British delimitation Commission in 1893. Major Grant was specially charged with the duty of fixing the longitude of the Niger sources. He proceeded to Kruto after the British Commission had left Tembi Kunda, travelling up from the coast by a different route from that we had followed. Finding that the moon would be too far advanced by the time he reached Tembi Kunda, he set up his transit instrument at Kruto, and from the mean of six moon culminations obtained a longitude of 11° 15′ 20″. With this longitude, and with the latitude obtained by the British Commission of 9° 6′ 25″, mean of four observations — the previously obtained latitude by Captain Compton being 9° 6′ 13″—the position of Kruto has been fixed on the map, and the traverse has been adjusted between this place and Bumban.

At Tembi Kunda Major Grant, carrying the time from Kruto with five watches, and returning at once to Kruto to check his rating, made the longitude by meridian distance 10° 46′ 33″ W. The British Commission with watches, assuming Major Grant's longitude for Kruto, made the longitude by meridian distance 10° 46′ 40″, and the French Commission by independent observations of lunar distances made it 10° 47′ 0″. The latitude obtained by the British Commission for their camp was 9° 5′ 20″ (mean of observations of two pairs of stars), and by the French for theirs was 9° 4′ 55″ by circum-meridian observations. The French camp was situated about a quarter of a mile south of the British camp, and the head of the Tembi ravine was about east of the interval between the two camps. For the map, therefore, the latitude of 9° 5′ 0″ and the longitude of 10° 47′ 0″ for the Niger sources have been accepted. Between this point and Kruto, as fixed before, the route traverse has been adjusted.

From Tembi Kunda to the 10th parallel of north latitude a triangulated survey was made and was closed north of Kalieri on a point fixed in latitude only. The three watches which were taken by the British Commissioners all proved untrustworthy after leaving Tembi Kunda, and the meridian distances obtained were manifestly very wrong. We had with us also Captain Hill's apparatus for obtaining the longitude by a series of instantaneous exposures of the moon, taken with a large camera on a solid stand, and by recording on the same negative the trails made by two stars having a declination within 5° of that of the moon. Captain Tyler managed the apparatus, and took and developed five excellent photographs, of which the first three were made at Bumban, at Mussadugu (near the watershed), and near Kalieri. The results, as calculated at home from these photographs, were, however, not satisfactory. and they were rejected in compiling the map. But the triangulation closed so nearly, as regards latitude, that, assuming Tembi Kunda to be rightly placed, any sensible error in the longitude of Kalieri is improbable, The triangulated points were, moreover, checked by magnetic bearings taken from every observing station. The longitude was further confirmed by that obtained for the terminal point of the next section of the survey.

The longitude of Kalieri, obtained by the triangulation from the position of Tembi Kunda, as fixed above, is approximately 11° 14′ W., or about 3½ miles east of the position given to it on the last published map. The only known observation for longitude there is one by Mr. Garrett in 1890, which makes it 11° 18′ 45″. But Mr. Garrett's longitudes are generally about 1′ west of Major Kenney's in the same district, and as both observers depended on watches, an error of from 1′ to 5′ is quite probable. There is collateral evidence, however, that the true longitude of Falaba and Kalieri is east of the positions previously assigned to them, as the general direction of the route from Kruto to Falaba could only be maintained by giving to the former place the longitude of 11° 18′ 58″, obtained by Captain Compton. Major Grant, however, has shown that the true longitude is

11° 15′ 20″, and therefore Koinadugu, placed by Captain Compton in 11° 25′ W. longitude, must be found about 3′ east of this position, and Falaba must be similarly 3′ east of the position shown on the last map, which exactly corresponds to the place it should occupy according to the triangulation.

The next section of the boundary survey extends from the intersection of the 10th parallel N. lat. with the watershed boundary to the intersection of the same parallel with the Kaba or Little Skarsies river. The work was done with theodolite and perambulator, the French Commissioners working with a theodolite compass, and measuring distances with a stadiometer.

An excellent photo. longitude was obtained by Captain Tyler at the Kaba river, which confirmed the perambulator distances, and also agreed most satisfactorily with the longitude for the other end of the section obtained by the triangulation. This observation places the Kaba river in longitude 11° 55′ 57″ W. The latitude was also checked at the same place by circum-meridian observations of two stars.

The next and last section of the survey ran from the Kaba river to the Great Skarsies or Kolinte at Wellia. For Wellia we had Major Kenney's longitude, 12° 33′ 57″, obtained by meridian distance from Freetown. Our own meridian distance gave to Wellia a longitude of 12° 35′ 35″, whilst a very good photograph by Captain Tyler brought the longitude to 12° 31′ 32″. A mean of these results has been adopted for the map. The latitudes found by circum-meridian observations of stars for the Kita-Lolo junction, 9° 52′ 40″, the point on the Kita river 1500 metres north of Lakhata, 9° 56′ 0″, and for Wellia, 9° 50′ 40″, have been adopted, and the survey has been adjusted on these points. The work of the French Commission from the junction of the 10th parallel and the Great Skarsies river was done independently, and was placed freely at our disposal by Captain Passaga. It strengthens the opinion formed by us as to the accuracy of the framework of points on which the survey has been adjusted, and considering the knowledge acquired by previous observers, and the assistance we had placed at our disposal from Major Grant and from the French Commissioners, it is probable that the error in the points forming the framework is limited to a possible 1′ of longitude.

On our journey coastwards from Wellia to Kambia, we made a route traverse, using prismatic compass and taking a mean of the distances paced by the five Europeans of our party. Astronomical observations were impossible, the sky being clouded every night, and, though we had a theodolite set up ready for use, we never succeeded in getting a star. We therefore accepted the position of Kukuna as given on previous maps, as in latitude 9° 23′ 55″, and longitude 12° 40′ 21″ W. This is taken from observations by Major Kenney, R.E., Mr. Garrett having fixed the town in 9° 23′ 45″ N. latitude, and 12° 45′ 20″ W. longitude. Between Kukuna as thus fixed and Wellia as given above our route traverse was adjusted. The distances agreed closely

# GEOGRAPHY AND TOPOGRAPHY

with those given on the map, and the ground being hard and the roads straight, we marched directly from point to point.

South of Kukuna survey work was suspended, as the route thence to Kambia is well known, and has been frequently traversed.

The advantage of the work done by the British and French Commissions, and by Sir F. Cardew's expedition, towards the future clearing up of the geography and topography of the Sierra Leone Protectorate and of the adjoining part of the Western Sudan is very great, not from any intrinsic merit of the work itself, but because of the direction taken by the expeditions. This will be at once apparent to any cartographer. By running a survey, adjusted on fixed points, completely round a country, a girdle of geographical information is made to encircle the land, and any routes from known points either inside or outside of the country can be easily adjusted as soon as they touch the frontier. Any one now can do great service with very little trouble by following with a prismatic compass the roads which run to the frontier from say Yana, Saionia, Bafodeya, Falaba, and Kruto, and by connecting the towns whose position is not very accurately known with one or two well-known points. When this has been done, and when the great rivers of the eastern part of the Protectorate have been explored and traced from their known ends to their embouchures, the country will be as well known as any where no high-class survey exists. The work still to be done is necessary not for scientific purposes only, but even more for commercial purposes, in order that the buried cities may be unearthed and the productive capacity of the land may be realized. The world of trade is slow to recognize the commercial value of geographical exploration, possibly because it is not immediately paying, and possibly because it is just as likely to reveal the barrenness as the wealth of a country; but to attempt to develop a country without first making a thorough and scientific exploration of it from end to end, is to begin

# GEOGRAPHY AND TOPOGRAPHY 223

a task without the knowledge which is essential to make it a successful undertaking.

The heights recorded in the previous chapters are taken from the mean of two daily readings of an aneroid barometer, one of which was taken about mid-day or after the day's march, and the other early the next morning. The recorded barometer readings give probably a very close approximation to the true heights above sea level, as there is remarkably little movement of the barometer due to atmospheric causes in West Africa in the dry season. When we remained several days in the same camp very little variation was recorded, and the occasional tornadoes hardly affected the barometer at all. Our aneroid was compared at sea level before we left the coast, and on our return it was again read. It was correct in the first case, but on our return read 200 feet at sea level. This was probably due to the commencing rainy season, and some small deduction may be necessary from the heights recorded after 1st May, but all these heights are so trifling that the correction required must be small. The French Commissioners also used an aneroid barometer, and on the two occasions when the same place was observed by both Commissions, the readings recorded were within 20 feet of each other.

As regards the general level of the interior, the flat country of the coast region covers a belt bounded by the east bank of the Great Skarsies (including the Samu country west of this river), from its mouth as far as its junction with the Kora, and up the Kora to a point some few miles north of Ula, where the hills of Tamisso begin. Turning eastward, the flat country includes Dunia, and turning south its border skirts the western side of the spur on which Kankuya is situated, and taking in the towns of Saionia, Dumbaia, Lakhata, Berea, makes for Bumban, and from thence reaches the coast by the valley of the Rokell river. Outside of this line the country in the northern half of the Protectorate has an altitude above sea level varying from 800 feet as a maximum, just north of Bumban, to 3300 feet near Tembi Kunda, the summits of the highest mountains

# GEOGRAPHY AND TOPOGRAPHY 225

being about 5000 feet. The highest ground is met with at the Niger sources, and about Wossu in Tamisso, the highest mountains seen being the Salu mountains, mounts Konkonante, Kenna, and the Kula peak, all near Tembi Kunda. The highest of the Tamisso mountains lie some distance north of the Anglo-French frontier. South of Tembi Kunda again are some considerable mountains, which are probably connected with the ranges about Waima.

The whole country which came within our notice is covered with high, dense vegetation, except only on the top of the spurs of the Tamisso mountains. The vegetation consists generally of scrub and cane brake, with occasional trees on the slopes and on the driest parts. It grows to a great height, much of it being far above a man's head, and it completely intercepts the view, and is very difficult to get through. All the valleys and waterlines are covered with a still denser vegetation, consisting of trees, creepers, and green bushes, and they are proportionately more difficult to cross. The dry bush may be burned in the dry season, but it will not burn well till about February. After the bush has been burned the ground is comparatively easy to traverse, but it is very seldom cleared except in patches by bush fires.

The instrument mainly used for astronomical work by our commission was a 6-inch transit theodolite reading to ten seconds. A 7-inch sextant was also occasionally used. Observations for latitude were generally made by meridian determinations of pairs of stars, and observations for time by the mean of determinations of at least two pairs of east and west stars. When the positions were specially important, latitudes were obtained from circummeridian observations, about eight pairs of observations being made, and each pair being worked out separately for latitude.

The French Commission carried a large theodolite reading to five seconds. Their observations for latitude were all circummeridian. We carried three deck watches, but found that they could not be depended

# GEOGRAPHY AND TOPOGRAPHY

upon except for giving the meridian distance between two places only a few days apart.

Our topographical work was done mainly with plane tables, and along the watershed was based on the trigonometrically fixed points. For the rest of the way the plane table was used in conjunction with the perambulator, and later with paced distances.

The compass bearings were taken with a large prismatic compass lent by the Admiralty. This compass was also used for ascertaining the variation by observation, and on the three occasions when this was done the results gave a variation of from 18° 12′ to 18° 20′ W.

## APPENDIX I

## ITINERARY.

| Place. | Date of Leaving. | Mean Height of Barometer. | Corresponding Altitude. | Thermometer Readings (Fahrenheit). | Hours of Reading Thermometer and Barometer. | Distance from last Halt. | Remarks. |
|---|---|---|---|---|---|---|---|
| | 1895. | Inches. | Feet. | Degrees. | | Miles. | |
| Freetown | 16 Dec. | 30.00* | — | — | — | — | * At sea level. |
| Port Lokko | 18 ,, | 29.875 | 125 | — | — | — | |
| Makanna | 19 ,, | 29.875 | 125 | — | — | 11 | |
| Dofunkuyin | 20 ,, | 29.77 | 220 | 82 | 11.30 a.m. | 12¼ | |
| Rotata | 21 ,, | 29.86 | 140 | 84 | 9.0 a.m. | 7½ | |
| Mapema | 22 ,, | 28.88 | 120 | 81 | 12.30 p.m. | 13 | |
| | | | | 70 | 5.15 a.m. | | |
| Kalangba | 23 ,, | 29.77 | 220 | 83 | 10.45 a.m. | 11½ | |
| | | | | 73 | 5.40 p.m. | | |
| Madina | 24 ,, | 29.85 | 150 | 83 | 11.15 a.m. | 10½ | |
| | | | | 73 | 5.30 a.m. | | |
| Bumban | 26 ,, | 29.65 | 327 | 83 | 11.30 a.m. | 11½ | Halted at Bumban 25th December. |
| | | | | 73½ | 7.0 a.m. | | |
| | | | | 73 | 5.30 a.m. | | |
| Kawana | 27 ,, | 29.10 | 825 | 78 | 10.15 a.m. | 7½ | |
| | | | | 72 | 5.30 a.m. | | |
| Kamange | 28 ,, | 29.24 | 700 | 78 | 10.35 a.m. | 9¼ | |
| | | | | 66 | 5.0 a.m. | | |
| Katimbo | 29 ,, | 28.55 | 1,380 | 67 | 8.30 a.m. | 5⅝ | |
| | | | | 72.5 | 5.30 a.m. | | |
| Lengekoro | 30 ,, | 28.45 | 1,450 | 82 | 4.40 p.m. | 11¼ | |
| | | 28.425 | 1,500 | | | | |
| | | 28.4 | 1,500 | 73.5 | 5.0 a.m. | | |

# ITINERARY

| Place | Date | | | | | | Notes |
|---|---|---|---|---|---|---|---|
| Kundembaia | 31 Dec. | 28.8 | 1,100 | 84.5 | 12.30 p.m. | $11\frac{1}{8}$ | |
| | | 28.73 | 1,100 | 66 | 5.0 a.m. | | |
| | 1896. | | | | | | |
| Isaia | 1 Jan. | 28.75 | 1,100 | 68 | 11.45 a.m. | $8\frac{7}{8}$ | |
| | | 28.70 | 1,100 | 58 | 5.0 a.m. | | |
| Yerembo | 2 ,, | 28.30 | 1,600 | 69 | 11.45 a.m. | $10\frac{1}{2}$ | |
| | | 28.25 | 1,630 | 68.5 | 5.0 a.m. | | |
| Alkallia | 3 ,, | 28.60 | 1,300 | 72 | 10.15 a.m. | $9\frac{5}{8}$ | |
| | | 28.55 | 1,350 | 69 | 5.15 a.m. | | |
| Kilela | 4 ,, | 28.50 | 1,400 | 74 | 11.0 a.m. | $10\frac{1}{2}$ | |
| Kruto | 7 ,, | 28.725 | 1,200 | 78.5 | 9.30 a.m. | 9 | Halted at Kruto 5th and 6th January. |
| | | 28.75 | 1,150 | 78 | 8.0 a.m. | | |
| | | 28.775 | 1,125 | 69 | 8.0 a.m. | | |
| | | 28.725 | 1,175 | 68 | 5.30 a.m. | | |
| Nyedu | 8 ,, | 28.55 | 1,350 | 78 | 11.45 a.m. | $11\frac{3}{4}$ | |
| | | 28.55 | 1,350 | 68 | 5.20 a.m. | | |
| Sogurella | 9 ,, | 27.95 | 1,940 | 70 | 10.15 a.m. | $9\frac{1}{2}$ | |
| | | 27.94 | 2,000 | 70 | 5.20 a.m. | | |
| Kurubundo | 10 ,, | 28.24 | 1,700 | 72 | 9.0 a.m. | $5\frac{7}{8}$ | |
| | | 28.15 | 1,720 | 70 | 5.30 a.m. | | |
| Porpor | 11 ,, | 28.125 | 1,800 | 80 | 11.0 a.m. | $11\frac{1}{8}$ | |
| | | 28.12 | 1,860 | 72 | 5.30 a.m. | | |
| Buria | 12 ,, | 28.45 | 1,450 | 73.5 | 9.30 a.m. | $7\frac{7}{8}$ | |
| | | 28.35 | 1,550 | 71 | 5.30 a.m. | | |
| Kamindu | 13 ,, | 27.675 | 2,200 | 74 | 9.15 a.m. | 14 | |
| | | 27.525 | 2,300 | 72 | 5.20 a.m. | | |
| Tembi Kunda | 19 ,, | 27.175 | 2,750 | 78 | 11.0 a.m. | $5\frac{1}{4}$ | 14th, 15th, 16th, 17th, and 18th January halted at Tembi Kunda. |
| | | 27.05 | 2,850 | 69.5 | 6.30 a.m. | | |
| | | 27.1 | 2,800 | 70 | 7.0 a.m. | | |

# APPENDIX I

| Place. | Date of Leaving. | Mean Height of Barometer. | Corresponding Altitude. | Thermometer Readings (Fahrenheit). | Hours of Reading Thermometer and Barometer. | Distance from last Halt. | Remarks. |
|---|---|---|---|---|---|---|---|
| | 1896. | Inches. | Feet. | Degrees. | | Miles. | |
| Camp I. | 21 Jan. | 27.275 | 2,600 | 72 | 8.43 a.m. | 3½ | Halted 20th at Camp I. |
| | | 27.23 | 2,675 | 70 | 6.30 a.m. | | |
| Camp II. | 22 ,, | 27.35 | 2,520 | 79 | 11.0 a.m. | 3¼ | |
| | | 27.35 | 2,520 | 70 | 6.0 a.m. | | |
| Camp III. | 24 ,, | 27.30 | 2,580 | 83 | 12.0 noon | 3 | Halted 23rd January at Camp III. Tornado at night 22nd and 23rd January. |
| Bali | 26 ,, | 28.00 | 1,900 | 76 | 11.45 a.m. | 6 | Halted 25th at Bali. |
| | | 28.05 | 1,850 | 74 | 6.0 a.m. | | |
| | | 28.00 | 1,800 | 75 | 6.0 a.m. | | |
| Kulakoia | 27 ,, | 27.825 | 2,080 | 79 | 11.45 a.m. | 4 | |
| | | 27.75 | 2,020 | 58 | 7.0 a.m. | | |
| Samaindu | 29 ,, | 27.60 | 2,250 | 67 | 12.0 noon | 3¾ | Halted 28th January at Samaindu. |
| | | 27.60 | 2,250 | 67 | 6.30 a.m. | | |
| Yaraia | 30 ,, | 28.00 | 1,900 | 80 | 4.0 p.m. | 2½ | |
| | | 28.00 | 1,900 | 65 | 6.0 a.m. | | |
| Dandafarra | 31 ,, | 27.95 | 1,900 | 71 | 9.45 a.m. | 2¾ | |
| | | 27.90 | 2,000 | 64 | 6.0 a.m. | | |
| Boria | 2 Feb. | 27.65 | 2,225 | 86 | 12.30 p.m. | 4¼ | Halted 1st February at Boria. |
| | | 27.65 | 2,200 | 74 | 6.0 a.m. | | |

# ITINERARY

| | Date | | | | | | |
|---|---|---|---|---|---|---|---|
| Mussadugu | 4 Feb. | 27.65 | 2,200 | 76 | 11.0 a.m. | 4¼ | |
| | 6 „ | 27.625 | 2,250 | 70 | 6.30 a.m. | 3 | Halted 3rd February at Mussadugu. |
| Kirimandugu | | 28.25 | 1,650 | 75 | 10.0 a.m. | | Halted 5th February at Kirimandugu. |
| | 7 „ | 28.15 | 1,775 | 64 | 5.30 a.m. | | |
| | | 28.225 | 1,675 | 60 | 6.30 a.m. | | |
| Konkekoro | | 28.25 | 1,650 | 86 | 12.0 noon | 3 | |
| | 8 „ | 28.25 | 1,650 | 65 | 6.30 a.m. | 3 | |
| Kiridugu | | 28.25 | 1,650 | 70 | 11.0 a.m. | 2 | |
| | 10 „ | 28.225 | 1,675 | 62 | 6.30 a.m. | | |
| Benekoro | | 28.15 | 1,775 | 72 | 12.0 noon | 4¼ | Halted 9th at Benekoro. |
| | 12 „ | 28.125 | 1,750 | 61.5 | 6.30 a.m. | | |
| Farama | | 28.19 | 1,700 | 80.5 | 11.30 a.m. | 3½ | Halted 11th February at Farama. |
| | 14 „ | 28.225 | 1,675 | 63 | 6.30 a.m. | | |
| | | 28.25 | 1,650 | 66 | 6.30 a.m. | | |
| Camp IV. | | 28.275 | 1,625 | 79 | 11.0 a.m. | 3½ | Halted 13th February at Camp IV. |
| | 16 „ | 28.15 | 1,750 | 61 | 6.30 a.m. | | |
| | | 28.20 | 1,700 | 58 | 6.30 a.m. | | |
| Camp V. | | 28.175 | 1,750 | 72 | 10.0 a.m. | 2¾ | Halted on 15th at Camp V. |
| | 17 „ | 28.20 | 1,700 | 72 | 8.0 a.m. | | |
| | | 28.20 | 1,700 | 69 | 6.0 a.m. | | |
| Camp VI. at Old Karafaia (destroyed) | | 28.225 | 1,675 | 75 | 9.0 a.m. | 3½ | |
| | 18 „ | 28.175 | 1,725 | 70 | 6.0 a.m. | | |
| Morifinia | | 28.30 | 1,600 | 76 | 11.0 a.m. | 5 | |
| | 19 „ | 28.25 | 1,650 | 70 | 6.0 a.m. | | |
| Bonbonkoro | | 28.20 | 1,700 | 86 | 5.0 p.m. | 2¼ | |
| | 20 „ | 28.20 | 1,700 | 71 | 6.0 a.m. | | |
| Boala Karafaia | | 28.30 | 1,600 | 87 | 12.0 noon | 10 | Tornado during night of 19th February. |
| | 22 „ | 28.275 | 1,625 | 74 | 6.0 a.m. | | |
| Dakolofe | | 28.45 | 1,450 | 78 | 11.0 a.m. | 4 | Halted 21st at Dakolofe. |

# APPENDIX I

| Place. | Date of Leaving. | Mean Height of Barometer. | Corresponding Altitude. | Thermometer Readings (Fahrenheit). | Hours of Reading Thermometer and Barometer. | Distance from last Halt. | Remarks. |
|---|---|---|---|---|---|---|---|
| | 1896. | Inches. | Feet. | Degrees. | | Miles. | |
| Dakolofe (*cont.*) | 22 Feb. | 28.40 | 1,500 | 75 | 6.0 a.m. | | |
| | | 28.35 | 1,550 | 70 | 6.0 a.m. | | Tornadoes on night of 22nd and morning of 23rd February. |
| Salamaia | 23 ,, | 28.35 | 1,550 | 78 | 10.0 a.m. | 5½ | |
| | | 28.35 | 1,500 | 71 | 6.0 a.m. | | |
| Songoia | 24 ,, | 28.40 | 1,500 | 82 | 11.30 a.m. | 7¼ | |
| | | 28.30 | 1,600 | 69 | 6.30 a.m. | | |
| Kambaia | 25 ,, | 28.225 | 1,675 | 90 | 5.0 p.m. | 8½ | |
| | | 28.30 | 1,600 | 74 | 6.30 a.m. | | |
| Sanaia | 26 ,, | 28.175 | 1,700 | 91 | 5.30 p.m. | 8½ | |
| | | 28.25 | 1,650 | 71.5 | 6.30 a.m. | | |
| Berea Futambu | 27 ,, | 28.25 | 1,650 | 81 | 11.0 a.m. | 3 | |
| | | 28.20 | 1,700 | 69 | 7.0 a.m. | | |
| Kalieri | 3 Mar. | 28.14 | 1,750 | 83 | 6.0 p.m. | 8¾ | Halted at Kalieri 28th and 29th February and 1st and 2nd March. |
| | | 28.20 | 1,700 | 72 | 6.0 a.m. | | |
| | | 28.20 | 1,700 | 70 | 6.30 a.m. | | |
| | | 28.15 | 1,750 | 71 | 6.30 a.m. | | |
| | | 28.175 | 1,720 | 72 | 6.0 a.m. | | |
| | | 28.25 | 1,675 | 75 | 6.0 a.m. | | |
| Camp VII. | 8 ,, | 28.325 | 1,575 | 75 | 10.0 a.m. | 3 | Halted 4th, 5th, 6th, 7th of March at Camp VII. |
| | | 28.25 | 1,675 | 73 | 7.0 a.m. | | Halted 9th, 10th, 11th March at Camp VIII. |
| Camp VIII. | 12 ,, | 28.25 | 1,650 | 71 | 7.30 a.m. | ¾ | |
| | | 28.05 | 1,850 | 84 | 8.0 p.m. | | |

# ITINERARY

| | | | | | | |
|---|---|---|---|---|---|---|
| Simitia | – | 13 Mar. | 28.25 | 1,650 | 86 | 3.0 p.m. | 10¾ |
| Camp IX. | – | 17 " | 28.15 | 1,750 | 75 | 6.0 a.m. | 2½ | Halted 14th, 15th, 16th at Camp IX. |
| Camp X. | – | 18 " | 28.15 | 1,750 | 76 | 6.30 a.m. | 7 |
| Camp XI. | – | 19 " | 28.00 | 1,900 | 73 | 6.30 a.m. | 3 |
| Camp XII. | – | 20 " | 28.20 | 1,700 | 86 | 6.0 a.m. | |
| | | | 28.25 | 1,650 | 63 | 6.30 a.m. | |
| Camp XIII. | – | 21 " | 27.95 | 1,950 | 95 | 2.30 p.m. | ¾ |
| | | | 28.00 | 1,900 | 67 | 6.0 a.m. | |
| Camp XIV. | – | 22 " | 28.10 | 1,800 | 93 | 5.0 p.m. | 3½ |
| | | | 28.15 | 1,750 | 72 | 6.0 a.m. | |
| Camp XV. | – | 23 " | 28.35 | 1,550 | 94 | 4.0 p.m. | 4 |
| | | | 28.40 | 1,500 | 69 | 6.0 a.m. | |
| Camp XVI. | – | 24 " | 27.90 | 2,000 | 86 | 6.0 p.m. | 4½ |
| | | | 27.95 | 1,950 | 68 | 6.0 a.m. | |
| Camp XVII. | – | 25 " | 28.20 | 1,700 | 94 | 5.0 p.m. | 3½ |
| | | | 28.20 | 1,700 | 72 | 6.30 a.m. | |
| Camp XVIII. | – | 26 " | 28.15 | 1,750 | 88 | 11.0 a.m. | 2 |
| Camp XIX. | – | 27 " | 28.10 | 1,800 | 74 | 6.0 a.m. | 4 |
| | | | 28.20 | 1,700 | 74 | 6.30 a.m. | |
| Camp XX. | – | 28 " | 28.10 | 1,800 | 90 | 5.0 p.m. | 5 | Tornado at night. |
| | | | 28.275 | 1,620 | 74.5 | 6.30 a.m. | |
| Camp XXI. (near Yomaia) | | 29 " | 28.30 | 1,600 | 83 | 4.45 p.m. | 5 |
| | | | 28.30 | 1,600 | 72.5 | 6.30 a.m. | |
| Camp XXII. (near Small Skarsies) | | 1 April | 28.45 | 1,450 | 95 | 4.0 p.m. | 3 | Halted 30th and 31st March at Camp XXII. |
| | | | 28.50 | 1,400 | 71 | 6.30 a.m. | |
| | | | 28.35 | 1,550 | 88 | 11.0 a.m. | |
| | | | 28.275 | 1,625 | 73 | 6.0 a.m. | |
| | | | 28.25 | 1,650 | 78 | 6.30 a.m. | |
| | | | 28.25 | 1,650 | 75 | 6.30 a.m. | |

# APPENDIX I

| Place. | Date of Leaving. | Mean Height of Barometer. | Corresponding Altitude. | Thermometer Readings (Fahrenheit). | Hours of Reading Thermometer and Barometer. | Distance from last Halt. | Remarks. |
|---|---|---|---|---|---|---|---|
| | 1896. | Inches. | Feet. | Degrees. | | Miles. | |
| Camp XXIII. | 2 April | 28.40 | 1,500 | 86 | 9.0 p.m. | 3 | |
| | | 28.40 | 1,500 | 74 | 6.30 a.m. | | |
| Camp XXIV. | 10 ,, | 29.20 | 750 | 93 | 5.0 p.m. | 3 | Halted 3rd, 4th, 5th, 6th, 7th, 8th, and 9th April at Camp XXIV. |
| | | 29.20 | 750 | 78 | 6.30 a.m. | | |
| | | 29.20 | 750 | 70 | 6.30 a.m. | | |
| | | 29.275 | 750 | 80 | 6.30 a.m. | | |
| | | 29.275 | 750 | 78 | 6.30 a.m. | | |
| | | 29.275 | 750 | 77 | 6.30 a.m. | | |
| | | 29.275 | 750 | 78.5 | 6.30 a.m. | | |
| | | 29.275 | 750 | 76 | 6.30 a.m. | | |
| | | 29.275 | 750 | 77 | 6.30 a.m. | | |
| Camp XXV. | 11 ,, | 28.90 | 900 | 78 | 6.30 a.m. | 4 | |
| Camp XXVI. | 12 ,, | 28.60 | 1,350 | 77 | 6.30 a.m. | 4¼ | |
| Camp XXVII. | 13 ,, | 29.00 | 825 | 78 | 6.30 a.m. | 4¾ | |
| Camp XXVIII. (Kita-Lolo Junction) | 15 ,, | 29.35 | 650 | 78.5 | 6.30 a.m. | 5 | Halted 14th at Camp XXVIII. |
| | | 29.40 | 600 | 79 | 6.0 a.m. | | |
| Camp XXIX. (near Lakhata) | 16 ,, | 29.25 | 700 | 100 | 3.0 p.m. | 12 | |
| | | 29.35 | 650 | 79 | 6.0 a.m. | | |
| Camp XXX. | 18 ,, | 28.65 | 1,250 | 76 | 6.30 a.m. | 1 | Halted 17th at Camp XXX. |
| | | 28.65 | 1,250 | 89 | 11.0 a.m. | | |
| | | 28.65 | 1,250 | 76 | 6.30 a.m. | | |

# ITINERARY

| Place | Date | | | | | | Remarks |
|---|---|---|---|---|---|---|---|
| Camp XXXI. | 21 April | 28.30 | 1,600 | 89 | 4.30 p.m. | $\frac{1}{2}$ | Halted 19th and 20th at Camp XXXI. |
| | | 28.325 | 1,575 | 72 | 6.30 a.m. | | |
| | | 28.325 | 1,575 | 72 | 6.30 a.m. | | |
| Camp XXXII. | 22 " | 28.35 | 1,550 | 73 | 6.30 a.m. | 3 | |
| Camp XXXIII. | 23 " | 28.65 | 1,250 | 75 | 3.0 p.m. | 7 | |
| | | 27.10 | 2,800 | 92 | 6.0 a.m. | | |
| | | 27.10 | 2,800 | 72 | | | |
| Kankuya | 24 " | 27.50 | 2,400 | 90 | 3.0 p.m. | $3\frac{1}{2}$ | A little rain during the night of 23rd April. A little rain during day of 24th April. |
| | | 27.575 | 2,300 | 75 | 6.30 a.m. | | |
| Camp XXXIV. | 25 " | 29.35 | 600 | 89 | 3.0 p.m. | $4\frac{1}{2}$ | |
| | | 29.40 | 560 | 77 | 6.0 a.m. | | |
| Camp XXXV. (banks of Great Skarsies) | 29 " | 29.60 | 360 | 84 | 6.30 a.m. | $9\frac{5}{8}$ | Halted 26th, 27th, and 28th at Camp XXXV. Rain during night of 27th, and heavy rain during the whole night of 28th. |
| | | 29.60 | 360 | 81 | 6.30 a.m. | | |
| | | 29.55 | 400 | 76 | 6.30 a.m. | | |
| Wellia | 1 May | 29.35 | 600 | 81 | 11.0 a.m. | 1 | Halted at Wellia 30th April. |
| | | 29.35 | 600 | 80 | 6.30 a.m. | | |
| | | 29.325 | 625 | 82 | 6.0 a.m. | | |
| Fodea | 2 " | 29.475 | 500 | 86.5 | 5.30 p.m. | 20 | |
| | | 29.50 | 450 | 81 | 6.0 a.m. | | |
| Kufuna | 3 " | 29.675 | 300 | 88 | 11.0 a.m. | $9\frac{3}{4}$ | |
| | | 26.60 | 380 | 78 | 6.0 a.m. | | |
| Kukuna | 4 " | 29.615 | 350 | 82 | 3.0 p.m. | 16 | |
| | | 29.70 | 300 | 76 | 6.0 a.m. | | |
| Pettifu | 5 " | 29.75 | 250 | 86 | 5.0 p.m. | 24 | *At sea level barometer read 200 feet. Possibly due to commencement of rainy season. |
| Massama | 5 " | * | Embarked for Freetown. | | | 8 | |

## APPENDIX II

### LIST OF PLACES ASTRONOMICALLY FIXED.

| Name. | Lat. (N.) | Remarks. | Long. (W.) | Remarks. |
|---|---|---|---|---|
| | ° ′ ″ | | ° ′ ″ | |
| Makanna - | 8 47 55 | Single meridian altitudes, allowing for error of parallax. | | |
| Mapema - | 8 58 15 | Do. (mean of 2). | | |
| Kalangba - | 9 1 10 | Do. (1 only). | | |
| Madina - | 9 5 20 | Do. (mean of 3) | | |
| Bumban - | 9 7 15 | Do. | 11 56 8 | Longitude of Freetown assumed to be 13° 14′ W. |
| Kawana - | 9 12 0 | Do. (mean of 2). | | |
| Kamange - | 9 17 35 | Mean of F.R. and F.L. meridian altitudes. | | |
| Katimbo - | 9 21 25 | Do. | | |
| Lengekoro - | 9 28 20 | Do. | | |
| Kundembaia - | 9 22 55 | Do. | | |
| Yerembo - | 9 13 25 | Mean of sextant and theodolite altitudes. | | |
| Alkallia - | 9 8 50 | Do. | | |
| Kilela - | 9 10 10 | Do. | | |
| Kruto - | 9 6 25 | Mean of 4 theodolite altitudes | 11 20 28.2 | Longitude of Bumban assumed as above. |
| Nyedu - | 9 6 35 | 2 meridian altitudes, F.R. and F.L. | | |
| Sogurella - | 9 11 0 | Meridian altitudes with sextant and with theodolite, allowing for error of parallax. | | |

# LIST OF PLACES

| Place | | | | | Observation | | | | Remarks |
|---|---|---|---|---|---|---|---|---|---|
| Kurubundo | 9 | 12 | 20 | Mean of 3 meridian altitudes | 11 | 1 | 50 | Meridian distance from Kruto assumed 11° 50′ 20″ W. |
| Porpor | 9 | 8 | 10 | Do. | | | | |
| Buria | 9 | 7 | 55 | Mean of 2 meridian altitudes. | | | | |
| Kamindu | 9 | 7 | 20 | Mean of 3 meridian altitudes. | | | | |
| Tembi Kunda | 9 | 5 | 20 | Mean of 4 meridian altitudes | 10 | 46 | 40 | Meridian distance Kruto assumed. |
| Bali | 9 | 12 | 10 | Mean of 2, allowing for error of parallax. | | | | |
| Mussadugu | 9 | 18 | 30 | Mean of 3, allowing for error of parallax | 10 | 47 | 0 | Meridian distance Tembi Kunda assumed. |
| Kiridugu | 9 | 22 | 15 | Mean of 3 (F.R. and F.L.). | | | | |
| Dakolofe | 9 | 41 | 25 | Do. | | | | |
| Songoia | 9 | 45 | 10 | 1 meridian altitude with sextant. | | | | |
| Bambaireya | 9 | 33 | 10 | Circum-meridian observations taken by Capt. Passaga. | | | | |
| Kalieri | 9 | 58 | 0 | Mean of 4 meridian altitudes. | | | | |
| Bibia | 10 | 0 | 5 | Mean of circum-meridian observations by French and English. | | | | |
| Junction of Rivers Kita and Lolo | 9 | 52 | 40 | Circum-meridian; time of transit calculated by mean of results. | | | | |
| Kita River, at point 1,500 mètres north of Lakhata | 9 | 56 | 0 | Circum-meridian; times as preceding. | | | | |

| Name. | Lat. (N.). | Remarks. | Long (W.). | Remarks. |
|---|---|---|---|---|
| | ° ′ ″ | | ° ′ ″ | |
| Wellia (Wulia) | 9 50 40 | Circum-meridian; time by observation | 12 35 35 | By meridian distance from Freetown. |
| Source of Faliko | 9 19 21 | Circum-meridian observations by Capt. Passaga. | | |
| Baraba | 9 46 10 | Do. | 11 55 57 | Photo. longitude, Capt. Hill's method. |
| Kaba River, on 10th parallel | - | - | 12 31 32 | Do. |
| Wellia | - | - | | |

GLASGOW: PRINTED AT THE UNIVERSITY PRESS BY
ROBERT MACLEHOSE AND CO.

# A CATALOGUE OF BOOKS AND ANNOUNCEMENTS OF METHUEN AND COMPANY PUBLISHERS : LONDON 36 ESSEX STREET W.C.

## CONTENTS

|  | PAGE |
|---|---|
| FORTHCOMING BOOKS, | 2 |
| POETRY, | 10 |
| BELLES LETTRES, | 11 |
| ILLUSTRATED BOOKS, | 13 |
| HISTORY, | 14 |
| BIOGRAPHY, | 16 |
| TRAVEL, ADVENTURE AND TOPOGRAPHY, | 18 |
| GENERAL LITERATURE, | 19 |
| SCIENCE, | 21 |
| PHILOSOPHY, | 22 |
| THEOLOGY, | 22 |
| LEADERS OF RELIGION, | 24 |
| FICTION, | 25 |
| BOOKS FOR BOYS AND GIRLS, | 34 |
| THE PEACOCK LIBRARY, | 35 |
| UNIVERSITY EXTENSION SERIES, | 35 |
| SOCIAL QUESTIONS OF TO-DAY, | 36 |
| CLASSICAL TRANSLATIONS, | 37 |
| EDUCATIONAL BOOKS, | 38 |

NOVEMBER 1897

November 1897.

# Messrs. Methuen's
## Announcements

## Poetry

**SHAKESPEARE'S POEMS.** Edited, with an Introduction and Notes, by GEORGE WYNDHAM, M.P. *Crown 8vo. Buckram.* 6s.

This is a volume of the sonnets and lesser poems of Shakespeare, and is prefaced with an elaborate Introduction by Mr. Wyndham.

**ENGLISH LYRICS.** Selected and Edited by W. E. HENLEY. *Crown 8vo. Buckram.* 6s.
Also 15 copies on Japanese paper. *Demy 8vo.* £2, 2s. *net.*

Few announcements will be more welcome to lovers of English verse than the one that Mr. Henley is bringing together into one book the finest lyrics in our language.

**NURSERY RHYMES.** With many Coloured Pictures. By F. D. BEDFORD. *Small 4to.* 5s.

This book has many beautiful designs in colour to illustrate the old rhymes.

**THE ODYSSEY OF HOMER.** A Translation by J. G. CORDERY. *Crown 8vo.* 7s. 6d.

## Travel and Adventure

**BRITISH CENTRAL AFRICA.** By Sir H. H. JOHNSTON, K.C.B. With nearly Two Hundred Illustrations, and Six Maps. *Crown 4to.* 30s. *net.*

CONTENTS.—(1) The History of Nyasaland and British Central Africa generally. (2) A detailed description of the races and languages of British Central Africa. (3) Chapters on the European settlers and missionaries; the Fauna, the Flora, minerals, and scenery. (4) A chapter on the prospects of the country.

**WITH THE GREEKS IN THESSALY.** By W. KINNAIRD ROSE, Reuter's Correspondent. With Plans and 23 Illustrations. *Crown 8vo.* 6s.

A history of the operations in Thessaly by one whose brilliant despatches from the seat of war attracted universal attention.

**THE BENIN MASSACRE.** By CAPTAIN BOISRAGON. With Portrait and Map. *Crown 8vo.* 3s. 6d.

This volume is written by one of the two survivors who escaped the terrible massacre in Benin at the beginning of this year. The author relates in detail his adventures and his extraordinary escape, and adds a description of the country and of the events which led up to the outbreak.

# Messrs. Methuen's Announcements

**FROM TONKIN TO INDIA.** By PRINCE HENRI OF ORLEANS. Translated by HAMLEY BENT, M.A. With 80 Illustrations and a Map. *Crown 4to.* 25s.

The travels of Prince Henri in 1895 from China to the valley of the Bramaputra covered a distance of 2100 miles, of which 1600 was through absolutely unexplored country. No fewer than seventeen ranges of mountains were crossed at altitudes of from 11,000 to 13,000 feet. The journey was made memorable by the discovery of the sources of the Irrawaddy. To the physical difficulties of the journey were added dangers from the attacks of savage tribes. The book deals with many of the burning political problems of the East, and it will be found a most important contribution to the literature of adventure and discovery.

**THREE YEARS IN SAVAGE AFRICA.** By LIONEL DECLE. With an Introduction by H. M. STANLEY, M.P. With 100 Illustrations and 5 Maps. *Demy 8vo.* 21s.

Few Europeans have had the same opportunity of studying the barbarous parts of Africa as Mr. Decle. Starting from the Cape, he visited in succession Bechuanaland, the Zambesi, Matabeleland and Masbonaland, the Portuguese settlement on the Zambesi, Nyasaland, Ujiji, the headquarters of the Arabs, German East Africa, Uganda (where he saw fighting in company with the late Major 'Roddy' Owen), and British East Africa. In his book he relates his experiences, his minute observations of native habits and customs, and his views as to the work done in Africa by the various European Governments, whose operations he was able to study. The whole journey extended over 7000 miles, and occupied exactly three years.

**WITH THE MOUNTED INFANTRY IN MASHONALAND.** By Lieut.-Colonel ALDERSON. With numerous Illustrations and Plans. *Demy 8vo.* 12s. 6d.

This is an account of the military operations in Mashonaland by the officer who commanded the troops in that district during the late rebellion. Besides its interest as a story of warfare, it will have a peculiar value as an account of the services of mounted infantry by one of the chief authorities on the subject.

**THE HILL OF THE GRACES: OR, THE GREAT STONE TEMPLES OF TRIPOLI.** By H. S. COWPER, F.S.A. With Maps, Plans, and 75 Illustrations. *Demy 8vo.* 10s. 6d.

A record of two journeys through Tripoli in 1895 and 1896. The book treats of a remarkable series of megalithic temples which have hitherto been uninvestigated, and contains a large amount of new geographical and archæological matter.

**ADVENTURE AND EXPLORATION IN AFRICA.** By Captain A. ST. H. GIBBONS, F.R.G.S. With Illustrations by C. WHYMPER, and Maps. *Demy 8vo.* 21s.

This is an account of travel and adventure among the Marotse and contiguous tribes, with a description of their customs, characteristics, and history, together with the author's experiences in hunting big game. The illustrations are by Mr. Charles Whymper, and from photographs. There is a map by the author of the hitherto unexplored regions lying between the Zambezi and Kafukwi rivers and from 18° to 15° S. lat.

## History and Biography

**A HISTORY OF EGYPT, FROM THE EARLIEST TIMES TO THE PRESENT DAY.** Edited by W. M. FLINDERS PETRIE, D.C.L., LL.D., Professor of Egyptology at University College. *Fully Illustrated. In Six Volumes. Crown 8vo. 6s. each.*

VOL. V. ROMAN EGYPT. By J. G. MILNE.

**THE DECLINE AND FALL OF THE ROMAN EMPIRE.** By EDWARD GIBBON. A New Edition, edited with Notes, Appendices, and Maps by J. B. BURY, M.A., Fellow of Trinity College, Dublin. *In Seven Volumes. Demy 8vo, gilt top. 8s. 6d. each. Crown 8vo. 6s. each. Vol. IV.*

**THE LETTERS OF VICTOR HUGO.** Translated from the French by F. CLARKE, M.A. *In Two Volumes. Demy 8vo. 10s. 6d. each. Vol. II. 1835-72.*

This is the second volume of one of the most interesting and important collection of letters ever published in France. The correspondence dates from Victor Hugo's boyhood to his death, and none of the letters have been published before.

**A HISTORY OF THE GREAT NORTHERN RAILWAY, 1845-95.** By C. H. GRINLING. With Maps and Illustrations. *Demy 8vo. 10s. 6d.*

A record of Railway enterprise and development in Northern England, containing much matter hitherto unpublished. It appeals both to the general reader and to those specially interested in railway construction and management.

**A HISTORY OF BRITISH COLONIAL POLICY.** By H. E. EGERTON, M.A. *Demy 8vo. 12s. 6d.*

This book deals with British Colonial policy historically from the beginnings of English colonisation down to the present day. The subject has been treated by itself, and it has thus been possible within a reasonable compass to deal with a mass of authority which must otherwise be sought in the State papers. The volume is divided into five parts:—(1) The Period of Beginnings, 1497-1650; (2) Trade Ascendancy, 1651-1830; (3) The Granting of Responsible Government, 1831-1860; (4) *Laissez Aller*, 1861-1885; (5) Greater Britain.

**A HISTORY OF ANARCHISM.** By E. V. ZENKER. Translated from the German. *Demy 8vo. 7s. 6d.*

A critical study and history, as well as a powerful and trenchant criticism, of the Anarchist movement in Europe. The book has aroused considerable attention on the Continent.

**THE LIFE OF ERNEST RENAN.** By MADAME DARMESTETER. With Portrait. *Crown 8vo. 6s.*

A biography of Renan by one of his most intimate friends.

**A LIFE OF DONNE.** By AUGUSTUS JESSOPP, D.D. With Portrait. *Crown 8vo. 3s. 6d.*

This is a new volume of the 'Leaders of Religion' series, from the learned and witty pen of the Rector of Scarning, who has been able to embody the results of much research.

MESSRS. METHUEN'S ANNOUNCEMENTS 5

OLD HARROW DAYS. By J. G. COTTON MINCHIN. *Crown 8vo.* 5s.

A volume of reminiscences which will be interesting to old Harrovians and to many of the general public.

## Theology

A PRIMER OF THE BIBLE. By Prof. W. H. BENNETT. *Crown 8vo.* 2s. 6d.

This Primer sketches the history of the books which make up the Bible, in the light of recent criticism. It gives an account of their character, origin, and composition, as far as possible in chronological order, with special reference to their relations to one another, and to the history of Israel and the Church. The formation of the Canon is illustrated by chapters on the Apocrypha (Old and New Testament); and there is a brief notice of the history of the Bible since the close of the Canon.

LIGHT AND LEAVEN : HISTORICAL AND SOCIAL SERMONS. By the Rev. H. HENSLEY HENSON, M.A., Fellow of All Souls', Incumbent of St. Mary's Hospital, Ilford. *Crown 8vo.* 6s.

### Devotional Series

THE CONFESSIONS OF ST. AUGUSTINE. Newly Translated, with an Introduction, by C. BIGG, D.D., late Student of Christ Church. With a Frontispiece. 18mo. 1s. 6d.

This little book is the first volume of a new Devotional Series, printed in clear type, and published at a very low price.

This volume contains the nine books of the 'Confessions' which are suitable for devotional purposes. The name of the Editor is a sufficient guarantee of the excellence of the edition.

THE HOLY SACRIFICE. By F. WESTON, M.A., Curate of St. Matthew's, Westminster. 18mo. 1s.

A small volume of devotions at the Holy Communion.

## Naval and Military

A HISTORY OF THE ART OF WAR. By C. W. OMAN, M.A., Fellow of All Souls', Oxford. *Demy 8vo. Illustrated.* 21s.

Vol. II. MEDIÆVAL WARFARE.

Mr. Oman is engaged on a History of the Art of War, of which the above, though covering the middle period from the fall of the Roman Empire to the general use of gunpowder in Western Europe, is the first instalment. The first battle dealt with will be Adrianople (378) and the last Navarette (1367). There will appear later a volume dealing with the Art of War among the Ancients, and another covering the 15th, 16th, and 17th centuries.

The book will deal mainly with tactics and strategy, fortifications and siegecraft, but subsidiary chapters will give some account of the development of arms and armour, and of the various forms of military organization known to the Middle Ages.

A SHORT HISTORY OF THE ROYAL NAVY, From Early Times to the Present Day. By DAVID HANNAY. Illustrated. 2 Vols. *Demy 8vo.* 7s. 6d. *each.* Vol. I.

This book aims at giving an account not only of the fighting we have done at sea, but of the growth of the service, of the part the Navy has played in the development of the Empire, and of its inner life.

THE STORY OF THE BRITISH ARMY. By Lieut.-Colonel COOPER KING, of the Staff College, Camberley. Illustrated. *Demy 8vo.* 7s. 6d.

This volume aims at describing the nature of the different armies that have been formed in Great Britain, and how from the early and feudal levies the present standing army came to be. The changes in tactics, uniform, and armament are briefly touched upon, and the campaigns in which the army has shared have been so far followed as to explain the part played by British regiments in them.

## General Literature

THE OLD ENGLISH HOME. By S. BARING-GOULD. With numerous Plans and Illustrations. *Crown 8vo.* 7s. 6d.

This book, like Mr. Baring-Gould's well-known 'Old Country Life,' describes the life and environment of an old English family.

OXFORD AND ITS COLLEGES. By J. WELLS, M.A., Fellow and Tutor of Wadham College. Illustrated by E. H. NEW. *Fcap. 8vo.* 3s. *Leather.* 4s.

This is a guide—chiefly historical—to the Colleges of Oxford. It contains numerous illustrations.

VOCES ACADEMICÆ. By C. GRANT ROBERTSON, M.A., Fellow of All Souls', Oxford. *With a Frontispiece.* *Fcap. 8vo.* 3s. 6d.

This is a volume of light satirical dialogues and should be read by all who are interested in the life of Oxford.

A PRIMER OF WORDSWORTH. By LAURIE MAGNUS. *Crown 8vo.* 2s. 6d.

This volume is uniform with the Primers of Tennyson and Burns, and contains a concise biography of the poet, a critical appreciation of his work in detail, and a bibliography.

NEO-MALTHUSIANISM. By R. USSHER, M.A. *Cr. 8vo.* 6s.

This book deals with a very delicate but most important matter, namely, the voluntary limitation of the family, and how such action affects morality, the individual, and the nation.

PRIMÆVAL SCENES. By H. N. HUTCHINSON, B.A., F.G.S., Author of 'Extinct Monsters,' 'Creatures of Other Days,' 'Prehistoric Man and Beast,' etc. With numerous Illustrations drawn by JOHN HASSALL and FRED. V. BURRIDGE. *4to.* 6s.

A set of twenty drawings, with short text to each, to illustrate the humorous aspects of pre-historic times. They are carefully planned by the author so as to be scientifically and archæologically correct and at the same time amusing.

## Messrs. Methuen's Announcements

THE WALLYPUG IN LONDON. By G. E. FARROW, Author of 'The Wallypug of Why.' With numerous Illustrations. *Crown 8vo.* 3s. 6d.

An extravaganza for children, written with great charm and vivacity.

RAILWAY NATIONALIZATION. By CLEMENT EDWARDS. *Crown 8vo.* 2s. 6d. [*Social Questions Series.*

## Sport

SPORTING AND ATHLETIC RECORDS. By H. MORGAN BROWNE. *Crown 8vo.* 1s. *paper;* 2s. *cloth.*

This book gives, in a clear and complete form, accurate records of the best performances in all important branches of Sport. It is an attempt, never yet made, to present all-important sporting records in a systematic way.

THE GOLFING PILGRIM. By HORACE G HUTCHINSON. *Crown 8vo.* 6s.

This book, by a famous golfer, contains the following sketches lightly and humorously written:—The Prologue—The Pilgrim at the Shrine—Mecca out of Season—The Pilgrim at Home—The Pilgrim Abroad—The Life of the Links—A Tragedy by the Way—Scraps from the Scrip—The Golfer in Art—Early Pilgrims in the West—An Interesting Relic.

## Educational

EVAGRIUS. Edited by PROFESSOR LÉON PARMENTIER of Liége and M. BIDEZ of Gand. *Demy 8vo.* 7s. 6d. .
[*Byzantine Texts.*

THE ODES AND EPODES OF HORACE. Translated by A. D. GODLEY, M.A., Fellow of Magdalen College, Oxford. *Crown 8vo. buckram.* 2s.

ORNAMENTAL DESIGN FOR WOVEN FABRICS. By C. STEPHENSON, of The Technical College, Bradford, and F. SUDDARDS, of The Yorkshire College, Leeds. With 65 full-page plates, and numerous designs and diagrams in the text. *Demy 8vo.* 7s. 6d.

The aim of this book is to supply, in a systematic and practical form, information on the subject of Decorative Design as applied to Woven Fabrics, and is primarily intended to meet the requirements of students in Textile and Art Schools, or of designers actively engaged in the weaving industry. Its wealth of illustration is a marked feature of the book.

ESSENTIALS OF COMMERCIAL EDUCATION. By E. E. WHITFIELD, M.A. *Crown 8vo.* 1s. 6d.

A guide to Commercial Education and Examinations.

**PASSAGES FOR UNSEEN TRANSLATION.** By E. C. MARCHANT, M.A., Fellow of Peterhouse, Cambridge; and A. M. COOK, M.A., late Scholar of Wadham College, Oxford: Assistant Masters at St. Paul's School. *Crown 8vo.* 3s. 6d.

This book contains Two Hundred Latin and Two Hundred Greek Passages, and has been very carefully compiled to meet the wants of V. and VI. Form Boys at Public Schools. It is also well adapted for the use of Honour men at the Universities.

**EXERCISES IN LATIN ACCIDENCE.** By S. E. WINBOLT, Assistant Master in Christ's Hospital. *Crown 8vo.* 1s. 6d.

An elementary book adapted for Lower Forms to accompany the shorter Latin primer

**NOTES ON GREEK AND LATIN SYNTAX.** By G. BUCKLAND GREEN, M.A., Assistant Master at the Edinburgh Academy, late Fellow of St. John's College, Oxon. *Cr. 8vo.* 3s. 6d.

Notes and explanations on the chief difficulties of Greek and Latin Syntax, with numerous passages for exercise.

**A DIGEST OF DEDUCTIVE LOGIC.** By JOHNSON BARKER, B.A. *Crown 8vo.* 2s. 6d.

A short introduction to logic for students preparing for examinations.

**TEST CARDS IN EUCLID AND ALGEBRA.** By D. S. CALDERWOOD, Headmaster of the Normal School, Edinburgh. In a Packet of 40, with Answers. 1s.

A set of cards for advanced pupils in elementary schools.

**HOW TO MAKE A DRESS.** By J. A. E. WOOD. Illustrated. *Crown 8vo.* 1s. 6d.

A text-book for students preparing for the City and Guilds examination, based on the syllabus. The diagrams are numerous.

## Fiction

**LOCHINVAR.** By S. R. CROCKETT, Author of 'The Raiders,' etc. Illustrated by FRANK RICHARDS. *Crown 8vo.* 6s.

**BYEWAYS.** By ROBERT HICHENS. Author of 'Flames,' etc. *Crown 8vo.* 6s.

**THE MUTABLE MANY.** By ROBERT BARR, Author of 'In the Midst of Alarms,' 'A Woman Intervenes,' etc. *Crown 8vo.* 6s.

**THE LADY'S WALK.** By Mrs. OLIPHANT. *Crown 8vo.* 6s.

A new book by this lamented author, somewhat in the style of her 'Beleagured City.'

## Messrs. Methuen's Announcements

**TRAITS AND CONFIDENCES.** By The Hon. EMILY LAWLESS, Author of 'Hurrish,' 'Maelcho,' etc. *Crown 8vo.* 6s.

**BLADYS.** By S. BARING GOULD, Author of 'The Broom Squire,' etc. Illustrated by F. H. TOWNSEND. *Crown 8vo.* 6s.
A Romance of the last century.

**THE POMP OF THE LAVILETTES.** By GILBERT PARKER, Author of 'The Seats of the Mighty,' etc. *Crown 8vo.* 3s. 6d.

**A DAUGHTER OF STRIFE.** By JANE HELEN FINDLATER, Author of 'The Green Graves of Balgowrie.' *Crown 8vo.* 6s.
A story of 1710.

**OVER THE HILLS.** By MARY FINDLATER. *Crown 8vo.* 6s.
A novel by a sister of J. H. Findlater, the author of 'The Green Graves of Balgowrie.'

**A CREEL OF IRISH STORIES.** By JANE BARLOW, Author of 'Irish Idylls.' *Crown 8vo.* 6s.

**THE CLASH OF ARMS.** By J. BLOUNDELLE BURTON, Author of 'In the Day of Adversity.' *Crown 8vo.* 6s.

**A PASSIONATE PILGRIM.** By PERCY WHITE, Author of 'Mr. Bailey-Martin.' *Crown 8vo.* 6s.

**SECRETARY TO BAYNE, M.P.** By W. PETT RIDGE. *Crown 8vo.* 6s.

**THE BUILDERS.** By J. S. FLETCHER, Author of 'When Charles I. was King.' *Crown 8vo.* 6s.

**JOSIAH'S WIFE.** By NORMA LORIMER. *Crown 8vo.* 6s.

**BY STROKE OF SWORD.** By ANDREW BALFOUR. Illustrated by W. CUBITT COOKE. *Crown 8vo.* 6s.
A romance of the time of Elizabeth

**THE SINGER OF MARLY.** By I. HOOPER. Illustrated by W. CUBITT COOKE. *Crown 8vo.* 6s.
A romance of adventure.

**KIRKHAM'S FIND.** By MARY GAUNT, Author of 'The Moving Finger.' *Crown 8vo.* 6s.

**THE FALL OF THE SPARROW.** By M. C. BALFOUR. *Crown 8vo.* 6s.

**SCOTTISH BORDER LIFE.** By JAMES C. DIBDIN. *Crown 8vo.* 3s. 6d.

# A LIST OF
# Messrs. Methuen's
## PUBLICATIONS

## Poetry

### RUDYARD KIPLING'S NEW POEMS

**Rudyard Kipling.** THE SEVEN SEAS. By RUDYARD KIPLING. *Third Edition. Crown 8vo. Buckram, gilt top.* 6s.

'The new poems of Mr. Rudyard Kipling have all the spirit and swing of their predecessors. Patriotism is the solid concrete foundation on which Mr. Kipling has built the whole of his work.'—*Times.*

'Full of passionate patriotism and the Imperial spirit.'—*Yorkshire Post.*

'The Empire has found a singer; it is no depreciation of the songs to say that statesmen may have, one way or other, to take account of them.'—*Manchester Guardian.*

'Animated through and through with indubitable genius.'—*Daily Telegraph.*

'Packed with inspiration, with humour, with pathos.'—*Daily Chronicle.*

'All the pride of empire, all the intoxication of power, all the ardour, the energy, the masterful strength and the wonderful endurance and death-scorning pluck which are the very bone and fibre and marrow of the British character are here.' —*Daily Mail.*

**Rudyard Kipling.** BARRACK-ROOM BALLADS; And Other Verses. By RUDYARD KIPLING. *Twelfth Edition. Crown 8vo.* 6s.

'Mr. Kipling's verse is strong, vivid, full of character. . . . Unmistakable genius rings in every line.'—*Times.*

'The ballads teem with imagination, they palpitate with emotion. We read them with laughter and tears; the metres throb in our pulses, the cunningly ordered words tingle with life; and if this be not poetry, what is?'—*Pall Mall Gazette.*

**"Q."** POEMS AND BALLADS. By "Q.," Author of 'Green Bays,' etc. *Crown 8vo. Buckram.* 3s. 6d.

'This work has just the faint, ineffable touch and glow that make poetry 'Q.' has the true romantic spirit.'—*Speaker.*

**"Q."** GREEN BAYS: Verses and Parodies. By "Q.," Author of 'Dead Man's Rock,' etc. *Second Edition. Crown 8vo.* 3s. 6d.

'The verses display a rare and versatile gift of parody, great command of metre, and a very pretty turn of humour.'—*Times.*

**E. Mackay.** A SONG OF THE SEA. By ERIC MACKAY, Author of 'The Love Letters of a Violinist.' *Second Edition. Fcap. 8vo.* 5s.

'Everywhere Mr. Mackay displays himself the master of a style marked by all the characteristics of the best rhetoric. He has a keen sense of rhythm and of general balance; his verse is excellently sonorous.'—*Globe.*

**Ibsen.** BRAND. A Drama by HENRIK IBSEN. Translated by WILLIAM WILSON. *Second Edition. Crown 8vo. 3s. 6d.*

'The greatest world-poem of the nineteenth century next to "Faust." It is in the same set with "Agamemnon," with "Lear," with the literature that we now instinctively regard as high and holy.'—*Daily Chronicle.*

**"A. G."** VERSES TO ORDER. By "A. G." *Cr. 8vo. 2s. 6d. net.*

A small volume of verse by a writer whose initials are well known to Oxford men.
'A capital specimen of light academic poetry. These verses are very bright and engaging, easy and sufficiently witty.'—*St. James's Gazette.*

## Belles Lettres, Anthologies, etc.

**R. L. Stevenson.** VAILIMA LETTERS. By ROBERT LOUIS STEVENSON. With an Etched Portrait by WILLIAM STRANG, and other Illustrations. *Second Edition. Crown 8vo. Buckram. 7s. 6d.*

'Few publications have in our time been more eagerly awaited than these "Vailima Letters," giving the first fruits of the correspondence of Robert Louis Stevenson. But, high as the tide of expectation has run, no reader can possibly be disappointed in the result.'—*St. James's Gazette.*

**Henley and Whibley.** A BOOK OF ENGLISH PROSE. Collected by W. E. HENLEY and CHARLES WHIBLEY. *Crown 8vo. 6s.*

'A unique volume of extracts—an art gallery of early prose.'—*Birmingham Post.*
'An admirable companion to Mr. Henley's "Lyra Heroica."'—*Saturday Review.*
'Quite delightful. A greater treat for those not well acquainted with pre-Restoration prose could not be imagined.'—*Athenæum.*

**H. C. Beeching.** LYRA SACRA : An Anthology of Sacred Verse. Edited by H. C. BEECHING, M.A. *Crown 8vo. Buckram. 6s.*

'A charming selection, which maintains a lofty standard of excellence.'—*Times.*

**"Q."** THE GOLDEN POMP : A Procession of English Lyrics from Surrey to Shirley, arranged by A. T. QUILLER COUCH. *Crown 8vo. Buckram. 6s.*

'A delightful volume : a really golden "Pomp."'—*Spectator.*

**W. B. Yeats.** AN ANTHOLOGY OF IRISH VERSE. Edited by W. B. YEATS. *Crown 8vo. 3s. 6d.*

'An attractive and catholic selection.'—*Times.*

**G. W. Steevens.** MONOLOGUES OF THE DEAD. By G. W. STEEVENS. *Foolscap 8vo. 3s. 6d.*

A series of Soliloquies in which famous men of antiquity—Julius Cæsar, Nero, Alcibiades, etc., attempt to express themselves in the modes of thought and language of to-day.
The effect is sometimes splendid, sometimes bizarre, but always amazingly clever —*Pall Mall Gazette.*

**Victor Hugo.** THE LETTERS OF VICTOR HUGO. Translated from the French by F. CLARKE, M.A. *In Two Volumes. Demy 8vo.* 10s. 6d. *each. Vol. I.* 1815-35.

This is the first volume of one of the most interesting and important collection of letters ever published in France. The correspondence dates from Victor Hugo's boyhood to his death, and none of the letters have been published before. The arrangement is chiefly chronological, but where there is an interesting set of letters to one person these are arranged together. The first volume contains, among others, (1) Letters to his father; (2) to his young wife; (3) to his confessor, Lamennais; a very important set of about fifty letters to Sainte-Beauve; (5) letters about his early books and plays.

'A charming and vivid picture of a man whose egotism never marred his natural kindness, and whose vanity did not impair his greatness.'—*Standard.*

**C. H. Pearson.** ESSAYS AND CRITICAL REVIEWS. By C. H. PEARSON, M.A., Author of 'National Life and Character.' Edited, with a Biographical Sketch, by H. A. STRONG, M.A., LL.D. With a Portrait. *Demy 8vo.* 10s. 6d.

'Remarkable for careful handling, breadth of view, and knowledge.'—*Scotsman.*
'Charming essays.'—*Spectator.*

**W. M. Dixon.** A PRIMER OF TENNYSON. By W. M. DIXON, M.A., Professor of English Literature at Mason College. *Crown 8vo.* 2s. 6d.

'Much sound and well-expressed criticism and acute literary judgments. The bibliography is a boon.'—*Speaker.*

**W. A. Craigie.** A PRIMER OF BURNS. By W. A. CRAIGIE. *Crown 8vo.* 2s. 6d.

This book is planned on a method similar to the 'Primer of Tennyson.' It has also a glossary.
'A valuable addition to the literature of the poet.'—*Times.*
'An excellent short account.'—*Pall Mall Gazette.*
'An admirable introduction.'—*Globe.*

**Sterne.** THE LIFE AND OPINIONS OF TRISTRAM SHANDY. By LAWRENCE STERNE. With an Introduction by CHARLES WHIBLEY, and a Portrait. 2 *vols.* 7s.

'Very dainty volumes are these; the paper, type, and light-green binding are all very agreeable to the eye. *Simplex munditiis* is the phrase that might be applied to them.'—*Globe.*

**Congreve.** THE COMEDIES OF WILLIAM CONGREVE. With an Introduction by G. S. STREET, and a Portrait. 2 *vols.* 7s.

'The volumes are strongly bound in green buckram, are of a convenient size, and pleasant to look upon, so that whether on the shelf, or on the table, or in the hand the possessor is thoroughly content with them.'—*Guardian.*

**Morier.** THE ADVENTURES OF HAJJI BABA OF ISPAHAN. By JAMES MORIER. With an Introduction by E. G. BROWNE, M.A., and a Portrait. 2 *vols.* 7s.

**Walton.** THE LIVES OF DONNE, WOTTON, HOOKER, HERBERT, AND SANDERSON. By IZAAK WALTON. With an Introduction by VERNON BLACKBURN, and a Portrait. 3s. 6d.

**Johnson.** THE LIVES OF THE ENGLISH POETS. By SAMUEL JOHNSON, LL.D. With an Introduction by J. H. MILLAR, and a Portrait. *3 vols.* 10s. 6d.

**Burns.** THE POEMS OF ROBERT BURNS. Edited by ANDREW LANG and W. A. CRAIGIE. With Portrait. *Demy 8vo, gilt top.* 6s.

This edition contains a carefully collated Text, numerous Notes, critical and textual, a critical and biographical Introduction, and a Glossary.

'Among the editions in one volume, Mr. Andrew Lang's will take the place of authority.'—*Times.*

**F. Langbridge.** BALLADS OF THE BRAVE: Poems of Chivalry, Enterprise, Courage, and Constancy. Edited, with Notes, by Rev. F. LANGBRIDGE. *Crown 8vo. Buckram.* 3s. 6d. *School Edition.* 2s. 6d.

'A very happy conception happily carried out. These "Ballads of the Brave" are intended to suit the real tastes of boys, and will suit the taste of the great majority.' —*Spectator.* 'The book is full of splendid things.'—*World.*

## Illustrated Books

**Jane Barlow.** THE BATTLE OF THE FROGS AND MICE, translated by JANE BARLOW, Author of 'Irish Idylls,' and pictured by F. D. BEDFORD. *Small 4to.* 6s. *net.*

**S. Baring Gould.** A BOOK OF FAIRY TALES retold by S. BARING GOULD. With numerous illustrations and initial letters by ARTHUR J. GASKIN. *Second Edition. Crown 8vo. Buckram.* 6s.

'Mr. Baring Gould is deserving of gratitude, in re-writing in honest, simple style the old stories that delighted the childhood of "our fathers and grandfathers." As to the form of the book, and the printing, which is by Messrs. Constable, it were difficult to commend overmuch. —*Saturday Review.*

**S. Baring Gould.** OLD ENGLISH FAIRY TALES. Collected and edited by S. BARING GOULD. With Numerous Illustrations by F. D. BEDFORD. *Second Edition. Crown 8vo. Buckram.* 6s.

'A charming volume, which children will be sure to appreciate. The stories have been selected with great ingenuity from various old ballads and folk-tales, and, having been somewhat altered and readjusted, now stand forth, clothed in Mr. Baring Gould's delightful English, to enchant youthful readers.'—*Guardian.*

**S. Baring Gould.** A BOOK OF NURSERY SONGS AND RHYMES. Edited by S. BARING GOULD, and Illustrated by the Birmingham Art School. *Buckram, gilt top. Crown 8vo.* 6s.

'The volume is very complete in its way, as it contains nursery songs to the number of 77, game-rhymes, and jingles. To the student we commend the sensible introduction, and the explanatory notes. The volume is superbly printed on soft, thick paper, which it is a pleasure to touch; and the borders and pictures are among the very best specimens we have seen of the Gaskin school.'—*Birmingham Gazette.*

**H. C. Beeching.** A BOOK OF CHRISTMAS VERSE. Edited by H. C. BEECHING, M.A., and Illustrated by WALTER CRANE. *Crown 8vo, gilt top.* 5s.

A collection of the best verse inspired by the birth of Christ from the Middle Ages to the present day. A distinction of the book is the large number of poems it contains by modern authors, a few of which are here printed for the first time.

'An anthology which, from its unity of aim and high poetic excellence, has a better right to exist than most of its fellows.'—*Guardian.*

# History

**Gibbon.** THE DECLINE AND FALL OF THE ROMAN EMPIRE. By EDWARD GIBBON. A New Edition, Edited with Notes, Appendices, and Maps, by J. B. BURY, M.A., Fellow of Trinity College, Dublin. *In Seven Volumes. Demy 8vo. Gilt top.* 8s. 6d. *each. Also crown 8vo.* 6s. *each. Vols. I., II., and III.*

'The time has certainly arrived for a new edition of Gibbon's great work.... Professor Bury is the right man to undertake this task. His learning is amazing, both in extent and accuracy. The book is issued in a handy form, and at a moderate price, and it is admirably printed.'—*Times.*

'The edition is edited as a classic should be edited, removing nothing, yet indicating the value of the text, and bringing it up to date. It promises to be of the utmost value, and will be a welcome addition to many libraries.'—*Scotsman.*

'This edition, so far as one may judge from the first instalment, is a marvel of erudition and critical skill, and it is the very minimum of praise to predict that the seven volumes of it will supersede Dean Milman's as the standard edition of our great historical classic.'—*Glasgow Herald.*

'The beau-ideal Gibbon has arrived at last.'—*Sketch.*

'At last there is an adequate modern edition of Gibbon.... The best edition the nineteenth century could produce.'—*Manchester Guardian.*

**Flinders Petrie.** A HISTORY OF EGYPT, FROM THE EARLIEST TIMES TO THE PRESENT DAY. Edited by W. M. FLINDERS PETRIE, D.C.L., LL.D., Professor of Egyptology at University College. *Fully Illustrated. In Six Volumes. Crown 8vo.* 6s. *each.*

    Vol. I. PREHISTORIC TIMES TO XVI. DYNASTY. W. M. F. Petrie. *Third Edition.*

    Vol. II. THE XVIIth AND XVIIIth DYNASTIES. W. M. F. Petrie. *Second Edition.*

'A history written in the spirit of scientific precision so worthily represented by Dr. Petrie and his school cannot but promote sound and accurate study, and supply a vacant place in the English literature of Egyptology.'—*Times.*

**Flinders Petrie.** EGYPTIAN TALES. Edited by W. M. FLINDERS PETRIE. Illustrated by TRISTRAM ELLIS. *In Two Volumes. Crown 8vo.* 3s. 6d. *each.*

'A valuable addition to the literature of comparative folk-lore. The drawings are really illustrations in the literal sense of the word.'—*Globe.*

'It has a scientific value to the student of history and archæology.'—*Scotsman.*

'Invaluable as a picture of life in Palestine and Egypt.'—*Daily News.*

**Flinders Petrie.** EGYPTIAN DECORATIVE ART. By W. M. FLINDERS PETRIE, D.C.L. With 120 Illustrations. *Crown 8vo.* 3s. 6d.

'Professor Flinders Petrie is not only a profound Egyptologist, but an accomplished student of comparative archæology. In these lectures, delivered at the Royal Institution, he displays both qualifications with rare skill in elucidating the development of decorative art in Egypt, and in tracing its influence on the art of other countries.'—*Times.*

**S. Baring Gould.** THE TRAGEDY OF THE CÆSARS. The Emperors of the Julian and Claudian Lines. With numerous Illustrations from Busts, Gems, Cameos, etc. By S. BARING GOULD, Author of 'Mehalah,' etc. *Fourth Edition. Royal 8vo.* 15s.

'A most splendid and fascinating book on a subject of undying interest. The great feature of the book is the use the author has made of the existing portraits of the Caesars, and the admirable critical subtlety he has exhibited in dealing with this line of research. It is brilliantly written, and the illustrations are supplied on a scale of profuse magnificence.'—*Daily Chronicle.*
'The volumes will in no sense disappoint the general reader. Indeed, in their way, there is nothing in any sense so good in English. ... Mr. Baring Gould has presented his narrative in such a way as not to make one dull page.'—*Athenæum.*

**H. de B. Gibbins.** INDUSTRY IN ENGLAND : HISTORICAL OUTLINES. By H. DE B. GIBBINS, M.A., D.Litt. With 5 Maps. *Second Edition. Demy 8vo.* 10s. 6d.

This book is written with the view of affording a clear view of the main facts of English Social and Industrial History placed in due perspective. Beginning with prehistoric times, it passes in review the growth and advance of industry up to the nineteenth century, showing its gradual development and progress. The book is illustrated by Maps, Diagrams, and Tables.

**A. Clark.** THE COLLEGES OF OXFORD : Their History and their Traditions. By Members of the University. Edited by A. CLARK, M.A., Fellow and Tutor of Lincoln College. *8vo.* 12s. 6d.

'A work which will certainly be appealed to for many years as the standard book on the Colleges of Oxford.'—*Athenæum.*

**Perrens.** THE HISTORY OF FLORENCE FROM 1434 TO 1492. By F. T. PERRENS. Translated by HANNAH LYNCH. *8vo.* 12s. 6d.

A history of Florence under the domination of Cosimo, Piero, and Lorenzo de Medicis.
'This is a standard book by an honest and intelligent historian, who has deserved well of all who are interested in Italian history.'—*Manchester Guardian.*

**J. Wells.** A SHORT HISTORY OF ROME. By J. WELLS, M.A., Fellow and Tutor of Wadham Coll., Oxford. With 4 Maps. *Crown 8vo.* 3s. 6d.

This book is intended for the Middle and Upper Forms of Public Schools and for Pass Students at the Universities. It contains copious Tables, etc.
'An original work written on an original plan, and with uncommon freshness and vigour.'—*Speaker.*

**E. L. S. Horsburgh.** THE CAMPAIGN OF WATERLOO. By E. L. S. HORSBURGH, B.A. *With Plans. Crown 8vo. 5s.*

'A brilliant essay—simple, sound, and thorough.'—*Daily Chronicle.*
'A study, the most concise, the most lucid, the most critical that has been produced. —*Birmingham Mercury.*

**H. B. George.** BATTLES OF ENGLISH HISTORY. By H. B. GEORGE, M.A., Fellow of New College, Oxford. *With numerous Plans. Third Edition. Crown 8vo. 6s.*

'Mr. George has undertaken a very useful task—that of making military affairs intelligible and instructive to non-military readers—and has executed it with laudable intelligence and industry, and with a large measure of success.'—*Times.*

**O. Browning.** A SHORT HISTORY OF MEDIÆVAL ITALY, A.D. 1250-1530. By OSCAR BROWNING, Fellow and Tutor of King's College, Cambridge. *Second Edition. In Two Volumes. Crown 8vo. 5s. each.*

> VOL. I. 1250-1409.—Guelphs and Ghibellines.
> VOL. II. 1409-1530.—The Age of the Condottieri.

'A vivid picture of mediæval Italy.'—*Standard.*
'Mr. Browning is to be congratulated on the production of a work of immense labour and learning.'—*Westminster Gazette.*

**O'Grady.** THE STORY OF IRELAND. By STANDISH O'GRADY, Author of 'Finn and his Companions.' *Cr. 8vo. 2s. 6d.*

'Most delightful, most stimulating. Its racy humour, its original imaginings, make it one of the freshest, breeziest volumes.'—*Methodist Times.*

# Biography

**S. Baring Gould.** THE LIFE OF NAPOLEON BONAPARTE. By S. BARING GOULD. With over 450 Illustrations in the Text and 12 Photogravure Plates. *Large quarto. Gilt top. 36s.*

'The best biography of Napoleon in our tongue, nor have the French as good a biographer of their hero. A book very nearly as good as Southey's "Life of Nelson."'—*Manchester Guardian.*
'The main feature of this gorgeous volume is its great wealth of beautiful photogravures and finely-executed wood engravings, constituting a complete pictorial chronicle of Napoleon I.'s personal history from the days of his early childhood at Ajaccio to the date of his second interment under the dome of the Invalides in Paris.'—*Daily Telegraph.*
'The most elaborate account of Napoleon ever produced by an English writer.'—*Daily Chronicle.*
'A brilliant and attractive volume. Never before have so many pictures relating to Napoleon been brought within the limits of an English book.'—*Globe.*
'Particular notice is due to the vast collection of contemporary illustrations.'—*Guardian.*
'Nearly all the illustrations are real contributions to history.'—*Westminster Gazette.*
'The illustrations are of supreme interest.'—*Standard.*

**Morris Fuller.** THE LIFE AND WRITINGS OF JOHN DAVENANT, D.D. (1571-1641), President of Queen's College, Lady Margaret Professor of Divinity, Bishop of Salisbury. By MORRIS FULLER, B.D. *Demy 8vo.* 10s. 6d.

'A valuable contribution to ecclesiastical history.'—*Birmingham Gazette.*

**J. M. Rigg.** ST. ANSELM OF CANTERBURY: A CHAPTER IN THE HISTORY OF RELIGION. By J. M. RIGG. *Demy 8vo.* 7s. 6d.

'Mr. Rigg has told the story of the great Primate's life with scholarly ability, and has thereby contributed an interesting chapter to the history of the Norman period.'—*Daily Chronicle.*

**F. W. Joyce.** THE LIFE OF SIR FREDERICK GORE OUSELEY. By F. W. JOYCE, M.A. With Portraits and Illustrations. *Crown 8vo.* 7s. 6d.

'This book has been undertaken in quite the right spirit, and written with sympathy insight, and considerable literary skill.'—*Times.*

**W. G. Collingwood.** THE LIFE OF JOHN RUSKIN. By W. G. COLLINGWOOD, M.A., Editor of Mr. Ruskin's Poems. With numerous Portraits, and 13 Drawings by Mr. Ruskin. *Second Edition.* 2 vols. 8vo. 32s.

'No more magnificent volumes have been published for a long time.'—*Times.*
'It is long since we had a biography with such delights of substance and of form. Such a book is a pleasure for the day, and a joy for ever.'—*Daily Chronicle.*

**C. Waldstein.** JOHN RUSKIN: a Study. By CHARLES WALDSTEIN, M.A., Fellow of King's College, Cambridge. With a Photogravure Portrait after Professor HERKOMER. *Post 8vo.* 5s.

'A thoughtful, impartial, well-written criticism of Ruskin's teaching, intended to separate what the author regards as valuable and permanent from what is transient and erroneous in the great master's writing.'—*Daily Chronicle.*

**W. H. Hutton.** THE LIFE OF SIR THOMAS MORE. By W. H. HUTTON, M.A., Author of 'William Laud.' *With Portraits. Crown 8vo.* 5s.

'The book lays good claim to high rank among our biographies. It is excellently, even lovingly, written.'—*Scotsman.*     'An excellent monograph.'—*Times.*

**Clark Russell.** THE LIFE OF ADMIRAL LORD COLLINGWOOD. By W. CLARK RUSSELL, Author of 'The Wreck of the Grosvenor.' With Illustrations by F. BRANGWYN. *Third Edition. Crown 8vo.* 6s.

'A book which we should like to see in the hands of every boy in the country.'—*St. James's Gazette.*     'A really good book.'—*Saturday Review.*

**Southey.** ENGLISH SEAMEN (Howard, Clifford, Hawkins, Drake, Cavendish). By ROBERT SOUTHEY. Edited, with an Introduction, by DAVID HANNAY. *Second Edition*. *Crown 8vo*. *6s*.

'Admirable and well-told stories of our naval history.'—*Army and Navy Gazette*.
'A brave, inspiring book.'—*Black and White*.

## Travel, Adventure and Topography

**R. S. S. Baden-Powell.** THE DOWNFALL OF PREMPEH. A Diary of Life with the Native Levy in Ashanti, 1895. By Colonel BADEN-POWELL. With 21 Illustrations and a Map. *Demy 8vo*. *10s. 6d*.

'A compact, faithful, most readable record of the campaign.'—*Daily News*.
'A bluff and vigorous narrative.'—*Glasgow Herald*.

**R. S. S. Baden-Powell.** THE MATEBELE CAMPAIGN 1896. By Colonel R. S. S. BADEN-POWELL. With nearly 100 Illustrations. *Second Edition*. *Demy 8vo*. *15s*.

'Written in an unaffectedly light and humorous style.'—*The World*.
'A very racy and eminently readable book.'—*St. James's Gazette*.
'As a straightforward account of a great deal of plucky work unpretentiously done, this book is well worth reading. The simplicity of the narrative is all in its favour, and accords in a peculiarly English fashion with the nature of the subject.' *Times*.

**Captain Hinde.** THE FALL OF THE CONGO ARABS. By SIDNEY L. HINDE. With Portraits and Plans. *Demy 8vo*. *12s. 6d*.

'The book is full of good things, and of sustained interest.'—*St. James's Gazette*.
'A graphic sketch of one of the most exciting and important episodes in the struggle for supremacy in Central Africa between the Arabs and their European rivals. Apart from the story of the campaign, Captain Hinde's book is mainly remarkable for the fulness with which he discusses the question of cannibalism. It is, indeed, the only connected narrative—in English, at any rate—which has been published of this particular episode in African history.'—*Times*.
'Captain Hinde's book is one of the most interesting and valuable contributions yet made to the literature of modern Africa.'—*Daily News*.

**W. Crooke.** THE NORTH-WESTERN PROVINCES OF INDIA: THEIR ETHNOLOGY AND ADMINISTRATION. By W. CROOKE. With Maps and Illustrations. *Demy 8vo*. *10s. 6d*.

'A carefully and well-written account of one of the most important provinces of the Empire. In seven chapters Mr. Crooke deals successively with the land in its physical aspect, the province under Hindoo and Mussulman rule, the province under British rule, the ethnology and sociology of the province, the religious and social life of the people, the land and its settlement, and the native peasant in his relation to the land. The illustrations are good and well selected, and the map is excellent.'—*Manchester Guardian*.

**W. B. Worsfold.** SOUTH AFRICA : Its History and its Future. By W. BASIL WORSFOLD, M.A. *With a Map. Second Edition. Crown 8vo.* 6s.

'An intensely interesting book.'—*Daily Chronicle.*
'A monumental work compressed into a very moderate compass.'—*World.*

## General Literature

**S. Baring Gould.** OLD COUNTRY LIFE. By S. BARING GOULD, Author of 'Mehalah,' etc. With Sixty-seven Illustrations by W. PARKINSON, F. D. BEDFORD, and F. MASEY. *Large Crown 8vo.* 10s. 6d. *Fifth and Cheaper Edition.* 6s.

'"Old Country Life, as healthy wholesome reading, full of breezy life and movement, full of quaint stories vigorously told, will not be excelled by any book to be published throughout the year. Sound, hearty, and English to the core.'—*World.*

**S. Baring Gould.** HISTORIC ODDITIES AND STRANGE EVENTS. By S. BARING GOULD. *Third Edition. Crown 8vo.* 6s.

'A collection of exciting and entertaining chapters. The whole volume is delightful reading.'—*Times.*

**S. Baring Gould.** FREAKS OF FANATICISM. By S. BARING GOULD. *Third Edition. Crown 8vo.* 6s.

'Mr. Baring Gould has a keen eye for colour and effect, and the subjects he has chosen give ample scope to his descriptive and analytic faculties. A perfectly fascinating book.'—*Scottish Leader.*

**S. Baring Gould.** A GARLAND OF COUNTRY SONG: English Folk Songs with their Traditional Melodies. Collected and arranged by S. BARING GOULD and H. FLEETWOOD SHEPPARD. *Demy 4to.* 6s.

**S. Baring Gould.** SONGS OF THE WEST: Traditional Ballads and Songs of the West of England, with their Traditional Melodies. Collected by S. BARING GOULD, M.A., and H. FLEETWOOD SHEPPARD, M.A. Arranged for Voice and Piano. In 4 Parts (containing 25 Songs each), *Parts I., II., III.,* 3s. each. *Part IV.,* 5s. *In one Vol., French morocco,* 15s.

'A rich collection of humour, pathos, grace, and poetic fancy.'—*Saturday Review.*

**S. Baring Gould.** YORKSHIRE ODDITIES AND STRANGE EVENTS. *Fourth Edition. Crown 8vo. 6s.*

**S. Baring Gould.** STRANGE SURVIVALS AND SUPERSTITIONS. With Illustrations. By S. BARING GOULD. *Crown 8vo. Second Edition. 6s.*

'We have read Mr. Baring Gould's book from beginning to end. It is full of quaint and various information, and there is not a dull page in it.'—*Notes and Queries.*

**S. Baring Gould.** THE DESERTS OF SOUTHERN FRANCE. By S. BARING-GOULD. With numerous Illustrations by F. D. BEDFORD, S. HUTTON, etc. *2 vols. Demy 8vo. 32s.*

'His two richly-illustrated volumes are full of matter of interest to the geologist, the archæologist, and the student of history and manners.'—*Scotsman.*

**G. W. Steevens.** NAVAL POLICY: WITH A DESCRIPTION OF ENGLISH AND FOREIGN NAVIES. By G. W. STEEVENS. *Demy 8vo. 6s.*

This book is a description of the British and other more important navies of the world, with a sketch of the lines on which our naval policy might possibly be developed. It describes our recent naval policy, and shows what our naval force really is. A detailed but non-technical account is given of the instruments of modern warfare—guns, armour, engines, and the like—with a view to determine how far we are abreast of modern invention and modern requirements. An ideal policy is then sketched for the building and manning of our fleet; and the last chapter is devoted to docks, coaling-stations, and especially colonial defence.

'An extremely able and interesting work.'—*Daily Chronicle.*

**W. E. Gladstone.** THE SPEECHES AND PUBLIC ADDRESSES OF THE RT. HON. W. E. GLADSTONE, M.P. Edited by A. W. HUTTON, M.A., and H. J. COHEN, M.A. With Portraits. *8vo. Vols. IX. and X. 12s. 6d. each.*

**J. Wells.** OXFORD AND OXFORD LIFE. By Members of the University. Edited by J. WELLS, M.A., Fellow and Tutor of Wadham College. *Crown 8vo. 3s. 6d.*

'We congratulate Mr. Wells on the production of a readable and intelligent account of Oxford as it is at the present time, written by persons who are possessed of a close acquaintance with the system and life of the University.'—*Athenæum.*

**L. Whibley.** GREEK OLIGARCHIES: THEIR ORGANISATION AND CHARACTER. By L. WHIBLEY, M.A., Fellow of Pembroke College, Cambridge. *Crown 8vo. 6s.*

'An exceedingly useful handbook: a careful and well-arranged study of an obscure subject.'—*Times.*

'Mr. Whibley is never tedious or pedantic.'—*Pall Mall Gazette.*

**L. L. Price.** ECONOMIC SCIENCE AND PRACTICE. By L. L. PRICE, M.A., Fellow of Oriel College, Oxford. *Crown 8vo.* 6s.

'The book is well written, giving evidence of considerable literary ability, and clear mental grasp of the subject under consideration.'—*Western Morning News.*

**C. F. Andrews.** CHRISTIANITY AND THE LABOUR QUESTION. By C. F. ANDREWS, B.A. *Crown 8vo.* 2s. 6d.

'A bold and scholarly survey.'—*Speaker.*

**J. S. Shedlock.** THE PIANOFORTE SONATA: Its Origin and Development. By J. S. SHEDLOCK. *Crown 8vo.* 5s.

'This work should be in the possession of every musician and amateur, for it not only embodies a concise and lucid history of the origin of one of the most important forms of musical composition, but, by reason of the painstaking research and accuracy of the author's statements, it is a very valuable work for reference.' —*Athenæum.*

**E. M. Bowden.** THE EXAMPLE OF BUDDHA: Being Quotations from Buddhist Literature for each Day in the Year. Compiled by E. M. BOWDEN. With Preface by Sir EDWIN ARNOLD. *Third Edition.* 16mo. 2s. 6d.

# Science

**Freudenreich.** DAIRY BACTERIOLOGY. A Short Manual for the Use of Students. By Dr. ED. VON FREUDENREICH. Translated from the German by J. R. AINSWORTH DAVIS, B.A., F.C.P. *Crown 8vo.* 2s. 6d.

**Chalmers Mitchell.** OUTLINES OF BIOLOGY. By P. CHALMERS MITCHELL, M.A., F.Z.S. *Fully Illustrated. Crown 8vo.* 6s.

A text-book designed to cover the new Schedule issued by the Royal College of Physicians and Surgeons.

**G. Massee.** A MONOGRAPH OF THE MYXOGASTRES. By GEORGE MASSEE. With 12 Coloured Plates. *Royal 8vo.* 18s. *net.*

'A work much in advance of any book in the language treating of this group of organisms. It is indispensable to every student of the Myxogastres. The coloured plates deserve high praise for their accuracy and execution.'—*Nature.*

## Philosophy

**L. T. Hobhouse.** THE THEORY OF KNOWLEDGE. By L. T. HOBHOUSE, Fellow and Tutor of Corpus College, Oxford. *Demy 8vo.* 21s.

'The most important contribution to English philosophy since the publication of Mr. Bradley's "Appearance and Reality." Full of brilliant criticism and of positive theories which are models of lucid statement.'—*Glasgow Herald.*

'An elaborate and often brilliantly written volume. The treatment is one of great freshness, and the illustrations are particularly numerous and apt.'—*Times.*

**W. H. Fairbrother.** THE PHILOSOPHY OF T. H. GREEN. By W. H. FAIRBROTHER, M.A., Lecturer at Lincoln College, Oxford. *Crown 8vo.* 3s. 6d.

This volume is expository, not critical, and is intended for senior students at the Universities and others, as a statement of Green's teaching, and an introduction to the study of Idealist Philosophy.

'In every way an admirable book. As an introduction to the writings of perhaps the most remarkable speculative thinker whom England has produced in the present century, nothing could be better.'—*Glasgow Herald.*

**F. W. Bussell.** THE SCHOOL OF PLATO: its Origin and its Revival under the Roman Empire. By F. W. BUSSELL, M.A., Fellow and Tutor of Brasenose College, Oxford. *Demy 8vo.* 10s. 6d.

'A highly valuable contribution to the history of ancient thought.'—*Glasgow Herald.*
'A clever and stimulating book, provocative of thought and deserving careful reading.'—*Manchester Guardian.*

**F. S. Granger.** THE WORSHIP OF THE ROMANS. By F. S. GRANGER, M.A., Litt.D., Professor of Philosophy at University College, Nottingham. *Crown 8vo.* 6s.

'A scholarly analysis of the religious ceremonies, beliefs, and superstitions of ancient Rome, conducted in the new instructive light of comparative anthropology.'—*Times.*

## Theology

**E. C. S. Gibson.** THE XXXIX. ARTICLES OF THE CHURCH OF ENGLAND. Edited with an Introduction by E. C. S. GIBSON, D.D., Vicar of Leeds, late Principal of Wells Theological College. *In Two Volumes. Demy 8vo.* 15s.

'The tone maintained throughout is not that of the partial advocate, but the faithful exponent.'—*Scotsman.*

'There are ample proofs of clearness of expression, sobriety of judgment, and breadth of view. ... The book will be welcome to all students of the subject, and its sound, definite, and loyal theology ought to be of great service.'—*National Observer.*

'So far from repelling the general reader, its orderly arrangement, lucid treatment, and felicity of diction invite and encourage his attention.'—*Yorkshire Post.*

**R. L. Ottley.** THE DOCTRINE OF THE INCARNATION. By R. L. OTTLEY, M.A., late fellow of Magdalen College, Oxon., Principal of Pusey House. *In Two Volumes. Demy 8vo.* 15s.

'Learned and reverent: lucid and well arranged.'—*Record.*
'Accurate, well ordered, and judicious.'—*National Observer.*
'A clear and remarkably full account of the main currents of speculation. Scholarly precision ... genuine tolerance ... intense interest in his subject—are Mr. Ottley's merits.'—*Guardian.*

**F. B. Jevons.** AN INTRODUCTION TO THE HISTORY OF RELIGION. By F. B. JEVONS, M.A., Litt.D., Principal of Bishop Hatfield's Hall. *Demy 8vo.* 10s. 6d.

Mr. F. B. Jevons' 'Introduction to the History of Religion' treats of early religion, from the point of view of Anthropology and Folk-lore; and is the first attempt that has been made in any language to weave together the results of recent investigations into such topics as Sympathetic Magic, Taboo, Totemism. Fetishism, etc., so as to present a systematic account of the growth of primitive religion and the development of early religious institutions.
'Dr. Jevons has written a notable work, and we can strongly recommend it to the serious attention of theologians, anthropologists, and classical scholars.'—*Manchester Guardian.*
'The merit of this book lies in the penetration, the singular acuteness and force of the author's judgment. He is at once critical and luminous, at once just and suggestive. It is but rarely that one meets with a book so comprehensive and so thorough as this, and it is more than an ordinary pleasure for the reviewer to welcome and recommend it. Dr. Jevons is something more than an historian of primitive belief—he is a philosophic thinker, who sees his subject clearly and sees it whole, whose mastery of detail is no less complete than his view of the broader aspects and issues of his subject is convincing.'—*Birmingham Post.*

**S. R. Driver.** SERMONS ON SUBJECTS CONNECTED WITH THE OLD TESTAMENT. By S. R. DRIVER, D.D., Canon of Christ Church, Regius Professor of Hebrew in the University of Oxford. *Crown 8vo.* 6s.

'A welcome companion to the author's famous 'Introduction.' No man can read these discourses without feeling that Dr. Driver is fully alive to the deeper teaching of the Old Testament.'—*Guardian.*

**T. K. Cheyne.** FOUNDERS OF OLD TESTAMENT CRITICISM: Biographical, Descriptive, and Critical Studies. By T. K. CHEYNE, D.D., Oriel Professor of the Interpretation of Holy Scripture at Oxford. *Large crown 8vo.* 7s. 6d.

This book is a historical sketch of O. T. Criticism in the form of biographical studies from the days of Eichhorn to those of Driver and Robertson Smith.
'A very learned and instructive work.'—*Times.*

**C. H. Prior.** CAMBRIDGE SERMONS. Edited by C. H. PRIOR, M.A., Fellow and Tutor of Pembroke College. *Crown 8vo.* 6s.

A volume of sermons preached before the University of Cambridge by various preachers, including the Archbishop of Canterbury and Bishop Westcott. A representative collection. Bishop Westcott's is a noble sermon.'—*Guardian.*

**E. B. Layard.** RELIGION IN BOYHOOD. Notes on the Religious Training of Boys. With a Preface by J. R. ILLINGWORTH. By E. B. LAYARD, M.A. 18mo. 1s.

**W. Yorke Faussett.** THE *DE CATECHIZANDIS RUDIBUS* OF ST. AUGUSTINE. Edited, with Introduction, Notes, etc., by W. YORKE FAUSSETT, M.A., late Scholar of Balliol Coll. *Crown 8vo.* 3s. 6d.

An edition of a Treatise on the Essentials of Christian Doctrine, and the best methods of impressing them on candidates for baptism.

'Ably and judiciously edited on the same principle as the ordinary Greek and Latin texts.'—*Glasgow Herald.*

## Devotional Books.

*With Full-page Illustrations. Fcap. 8vo. Buckram. 3s. 6d.*
*Padded morocco, 5s.*

THE IMITATION OF CHRIST. By THOMAS À KEMPIS. With an Introduction by DEAN FARRAR. Illustrated by C. M. GERE, and printed in black and red. *Second Edition.*

'Amongst all the innumerable English editions of the "Imitation," there can have been few which were prettier than this one, printed in strong and handsome type, with all the glory of red initials.'—*Glasgow Herald.*

THE CHRISTIAN YEAR. By JOHN KEBLE. With an Introduction and Notes by W. LOCK, D.D., Warden of Keble College, Ireland, Professor at Oxford. Illustrated by R. ANNING BELL.

'The present edition is annotated with all the care and insight to be expected from Mr. Lock. The progress and circumstances of its composition are detailed in the Introduction. There is an interesting Appendix on the MSS. of the "Christian Year," and another giving the order in which the poems were written. A "Short Analysis of the Thought" is prefixed to each, and any difficulty in the text is explained in a note.'—*Guardian.*

'The most acceptable edition of this ever-popular work.'—*Globe.*

## Leaders of Religion

Edited by H. C. BEECHING, M.A. *With Portraits, crown 8vo.*

A series of short biographies of the most prominent leaders of religious life and thought of all ages and countries.

**3/6**

The following are ready—

CARDINAL NEWMAN. By R. H. HUTTON.
JOHN WESLEY. By J. H. OVERTON, M.A.
BISHOP WILBERFORCE. By G. W. DANIEL, M.A.
CARDINAL MANNING. By A. W. HUTTON, M.A.
CHARLES SIMEON. By H. C. G. MOULE, M.A.
JOHN KEBLE. By WALTER LOCK, D.D.
THOMAS CHALMERS. By Mrs. OLIPHANT.
LANCELOT ANDREWES. By R. L. OTTLEY, M.A.
AUGUSTINE OF CANTERBURY. By E. L. CUTTS, D.D.
WILLIAM LAUD. By W. H. HUTTON, B.D.

MESSRS. METHUEN'S LIST

JOHN KNOX. By F. M'CUNN.
JOHN HOWE. By R. F. HORTON, D.D.
BISHOP KEN. By F. A. CLARKE, M.A.
GEORGE FOX, THE QUAKER. By T. HODGKIN, D.C.L.
Other volumes will be announced in due course.

# Fiction

### SIX SHILLING NOVELS
### Marie Corelli's Novels
*Crown 8vo. 6s. each.*

A ROMANCE OF TWO WORLDS. *Sixteenth Edition.*
VENDETTA. *Thirteenth Edition.*
THELMA. *Seventeenth Edition.*
ARDATH. *Eleventh Edition.*
THE SOUL OF LILITH *Ninth Edition.*
WORMWOOD. *Eighth Edition.*
BARABBAS: A DREAM OF THE WORLD'S TRAGEDY.
*Thirty-first Edition.*

'The tender reverence of the treatment and the imaginative beauty of the writing have reconciled us to the daring of the conception, and the conviction is forced on us that even so exalted a subject cannot be made too familiar to us, provided it be presented in the true spirit of Christian faith. The amplifications of the Scripture narrative are often conceived with high poetic insight, and this "Dream of the World's Tragedy" is, despite some trifling incongruities, a lofty and not inadequate paraphrase of the supreme climax of the inspired narrative.'—*Dublin Review.*

THE SORROWS OF SATAN. *Thirty-sixth Edition.*

'A very powerful piece of work. . . . The conception is magnificent, and is likely to win an abiding place within the memory of man. . . . The author has immense command of language, and a limitless audacity. . . . This interesting and remarkable romance will live long after much of the ephemeral literature of the day is forgotten. . . . A literary phenomenon . . . novel, and even sublime.'—W. T. STEAD in the *Review of Reviews.*

### Anthony Hope's Novels
*Crown 8vo. 6s. each.*

THE GOD IN THE CAR. *Seventh Edition.*

'A very remarkable book, deserving of critical analysis impossible within our limit; brilliant, but not superficial; well considered, but not elaborated; constructed with the proverbial art that conceals, but yet allows itself to be enjoyed by readers to whom fine literary method is a keen pleasure.'—*The World.*

A CHANGE OF AIR. *Fourth Edition.*

'A graceful, vivacious comedy, true to human nature. The characters are traced with a masterly hand.'—*Times.*

A MAN OF MARK. *Fourth Edition.*

'Of all Mr. Hope's books, "A Man of Mark" is the one which best compares with "The Prisoner of Zenda."'—*National Observer.*

**THE CHRONICLES OF COUNT ANTONIO.** *Third Edition.*
'It is a perfectly enchanting story of love and chivalry, and pure romance. The outlawed Count is the most constant, desperate, and withal modest and tender of lovers, a peerless gentleman, an intrepid fighter, a very faithful friend, and a most magnanimous foe.'—*Guardian.*

**PHROSO.** Illustrated by H. R. MILLAR. *Third Edition.*
'The tale is thoroughly fresh, quick with vitality, stirring the blood, and humorously, dashingly told.'—*St. James's Gazette.*
'A story of adventure, every page of which is palpitating with action and excitement.'—*Speaker.*
'From cover to cover "Phroso" not only engages the attention, but carries the reader in little whirls of delight from adventure to adventure.'—*Academy.*

### S. Baring Gould's Novels
*Crown 8vo. 6s. each.*

'To say that a book is by the author of "Mehalah" is to imply that it contains a story cast on strong lines, containing dramatic possibilities, vivid and sympathetic descriptions of Nature, and a wealth of ingenious imagery.'—*Speaker.*
'That whatever Mr. Baring Gould writes is well worth reading, is a conclusion that may be very generally accepted. His views of life are fresh and vigorous, his language pointed and characteristic, the incidents of which he makes use are striking and original, his characters are life-like, and though somewhat exceptional people, are drawn and coloured with artistic force. Add to this that his descriptions of scenes and scenery are painted with the loving eyes and skilled hands of a master of his art, that he is always fresh and never dull, and under such conditions it is no wonder that readers have gained confidence both in his power of amusing and satisfying them, and that year by year his popularity widens.'—*Court Circular.*

**ARMINELL: A Social Romance.** *Fourth Edition.*

**URITH: A Story of Dartmoor.** *Fifth Edition.*
'The author is at his best.'—*Times.*

**IN THE ROAR OF THE SEA.** *Sixth Edition.*
'One of the best imagined and most enthralling stories the author has produced.—*Saturday Review.*

**MRS. CURGENVEN OF CURGENVEN.** *Fourth Edition.*
'The swing of the narrative is splendid.'—*Sussex Daily News.*

**CHEAP JACK ZITA.** *Fourth Edition.*
'A powerful drama of human passion.'—*Westminster Gazette.*
'A story worthy the author.'—*National Observer.*

**THE QUEEN OF LOVE.** *Fourth Edition.*
'You cannot put it down until you have finished it.'—*Punch.*
'Can be heartily recommended to all who care for cleanly, energetic, and interesting fiction.'—*Sussex Daily News.*

**KITTY ALONE.** *Fourth Edition.*
'A strong and original story, teeming with graphic description, stirring incident, and, above all, with vivid and enthralling human interest.'—*Daily Telegraph.*

**NOÉMI: A Romance of the Cave-Dwellers.** Illustrated by R. CATON WOODVILLE. *Third Edition.*
'"Noémi" is as excellent a tale of fighting and adventure as one may wish to meet. The narrative also runs clear and sharp as the Loire itself.'—*Pall Mall Gazette.*
'Mr. Baring Gould's powerful story is full of the strong lights and shadows and vivid colouring to which he has accustomed us.'—*Standard.*

**THE BROOM-SQUIRE.** Illustrated by FRANK DADD. *Fourth Edition.*

'A strain of tenderness is woven through the web of his tragic tale, and its atmosphere is sweetened by the nobility and sweetness of the heroine's character.'—*Daily News.*

'A story of exceptional interest that seems to us to be better than anything he has written of late.'—*Speaker.*

**THE PENNYCOMEQUICKS.** *Third Edition.*

**DARTMOOR IDYLLS.**

'A book to read, and keep and read again; for the genuine fun and pathos of it will not early lose their effect.'—*Vanity Fair.*

**GUAVAS THE TINNER.** Illustrated by Frank Dadd. *Second Edition.*

'Mr. Baring Gould is a wizard who transports us into a region of visions, often lurid and disquieting, but always full of interest and enchantment.'—*Spectator.*

'In the weirdness of the story, in the faithfulness with which the characters are depicted, and in force of style, it closely resembles "Mehalah."'—*Daily Telegraph.*

'There is a kind of flavour about this book which alone elevates it above the ordinary novel. The story itself has a grandeur in harmony with the wild and rugged scenery which is its setting.'—*Athenæum.*

## Gilbert Parker's Novels
*Crown 8vo. 6s. each.*

**PIERRE AND HIS PEOPLE.** *Fourth Edition.*

'Stories happily conceived and finely executed. There is strength and genius in Mr. Parker's style.'—*Daily Telegraph.*

**MRS. FALCHION.** *Fourth Edition.*

'A splendid study of character.'—*Athenæum.*

'But little behind anything that has been done by any writer of our time.'—*Pall Mall Gazette.* 'A very striking and admirable novel.'—*St. James's Gazette.*

**THE TRANSLATION OF A SAVAGE.**

'The plot is original and one difficult to work out; but Mr. Parker has done it with great skill and delicacy. The reader who is not interested in this original, fresh, and well-told tale must be a dull person indeed.'—*Daily Chronicle.*

**THE TRAIL OF THE SWORD.** *Fifth Edition.*

'Everybody with a soul for romance will thoroughly enjoy "The Trail of the Sword."'—*St. James's Gazette.*

'A rousing and dramatic tale. A book like this, in which swords flash, great surprises are undertaken, and daring deeds done, in which men and women live and love in the old straightforward passionate way, is a joy inexpressible to the reviewer.'—*Daily Chronicle.*

**WHEN VALMOND CAME TO PONTIAC: The Story of a Lost Napoleon.** *Fourth Edition.*

'Here we find romance—real, breathing, living romance, but it runs flush with our own times, level with our own feelings. The character of Valmond is drawn unerringly; his career, brief as it is, is placed before us as convincingly as history itself. The book must be read, we may say re-read, for any one thoroughly to appreciate Mr. Parker's delicate touch and innate sympathy with humanity.'—*Pall Mall Gazette.*

'The one work of genius which 1895 has as yet produced.'—*New Age.*

**AN ADVENTURER OF THE NORTH: The Last Adventures of 'Pretty Pierre.'** *Second Edition.*

'The present book is full of fine and moving stories of the great North, and it will add to Mr. Parker's already high reputation.'—*Glasgow Herald.*

**THE SEATS OF THE MIGHTY.** *Illustrated. Eighth Edition.*
'The best thing he has done; one of the best things that any one has done lately.'—*St. James's Gazette.*
'Mr. Parker seems to become stronger and easier with every serious novel that he attempts. . . . In "The Seats of the Mighty" he shows the matured power which his former novels have led us to expect, and has produced a really fine historical novel. . . . Most sincerely is Mr. Parker to be congratulated on the finest novel he has yet written.'—*Athenæum.*
'Mr. Parker's latest book places him in the front rank of living novelists. "The Seats of the Mighty" is a great book.'—*Black and White.*
'One of the strongest stories of historical interest and adventure that we have read for many a day. . . . A notable and successful book.'—*Speaker.*

---

**Conan Doyle.** ROUND THE RED LAMP. By A. CONAN DOYLE, Author of 'The White Company,' 'The Adventures of Sherlock Holmes,' etc. *Fifth Edition. Crown 8vo. 6s.*
'The book is, indeed, composed of leaves from life, and is far and away the best view that has been vouchsafed us behind the scenes of the consulting-room. It is very superior to "The Diary of a late Physician."'—*Illustrated London News.*

**Stanley Weyman.** UNDER THE RED ROBE. By STANLEY WEYMAN, Author of 'A Gentleman of France.' With Twelve Illustrations by R. Caton Woodville. *Twelfth Edition. Crown 8vo. 6s.*
'A book of which we have read every word for the sheer pleasure of reading, and which we put down with a pang that we cannot forget it all and start again.'—*Westminster Gazette.*
'Every one who reads books at all must read this thrilling romance, from the first page of which to the last the breathless reader is haled along. An inspiration of "manliness and courage."'—*Daily Chronicle.*

**Lucas Malet.** THE WAGES OF SIN. By LUCAS MALET. *Thirteenth Edition. Crown 8vo. 6s.*

**Lucas Malet.** THE CARISSIMA. By LUCAS MALET, Author of 'The Wages of Sin,' etc. *Third Edition. Crown 8vo. 6s.*

**Arthur Morrison.** TALES OF MEAN STREETS. By ARTHUR MORRISON. *Fourth Edition. Crown 8vo. 6s.*
'Told with consummate art and extraordinary detail. He tells a plain, unvarnished tale, and the very truth of it makes for beauty. In the true humanity of the book lies its justification, the permanence of its interest, and its indubitable triumph.'—*Athenæum.*
'A great book. The author's method is amazingly effective, and produces a thrilling sense of reality. The writer lays upon us a master hand. The book is simply appalling and irresistible in its interest. It is humorous also; without humour it would not make the mark it is certain to make.'—*World.*

**Arthur Morrison.** A CHILD OF THE JAGO. By ARTHUR MORRISON. *Third Edition. Crown 8vo. 6s.*
This, the first long story which Mr. Morrison has written, is like his remarkable 'Tales of Mean Streets,' a realistic study of East End life.
'The book is a masterpiece.'—*Pall Mall Gazette.*
'Told with great vigour and powerful simplicity.'—*Athenæum.*

**Mrs. Clifford.** A FLASH OF SUMMER. By Mrs. W. K. CLIFFORD, Author of 'Aunt Anne,' etc. *Second Edition. Crown 8vo. 6s.*
'The story is a very sad and a very beautiful one, exquisitely told, and enriched with many subtle touches of wise and tender insight. It will, undoubtedly, add to its author's reputation—already high—in the ranks of novelists.'—*Speaker.*

**Emily Lawless.** HURRISH. By the Honble. EMILY LAW-LESS, Author of 'Maelcho,' etc. *Fifth Edition. Crown 8vo.* 6s.

A reissue of Miss Lawless' most popular novel, uniform with 'Maelcho.'

**Emily Lawless.** MAELCHO: a Sixteenth Century Romance. By the Honble. EMILY LAWLESS. *Second Edition. Crown 8vo.* 6s.

'A really great book.'—*Spectator.*
'There is no keener pleasure in life than the recognition of genius. Good work is commoner than it used to be, but the best is as rare as ever. All the more gladly, therefore, do we welcome in " Maelcho " a piece of work of the first order, which we do not hesitate to describe as one of the most remarkable literary achievements of this generation. Miss Lawless is possessed of the very essence of historical genius.'—*Manchester Guardian.*

**J. H. Findlater.** THE GREEN GRAVES OF BALGOWRIE. By JANE H. FINDLATER. *Fourth Edition. Crown 8vo.* 6s.

'A powerful and vivid story.'—*Standard.*
'A beautiful story, sad and strange as truth itself.'—*Vanity Fair.*
'A work of remarkable interest and originality.'—*National Observer.*
'A very charming and pathetic tale.'—*Pall Mall Gazette.*
'A singularly original, clever, and beautiful story.'—*Guardian.*
'"The Green Graves of Balgowrie" reveals to us a new Scotch writer of undoubted faculty and reserve force.'—*Spectator.*
'An exquisite idyll, delicate, affecting, and beautiful.'—*Black and White.*

**H. G. Wells.** THE STOLEN BACILLUS, and other Stories. By H. G. WELLS, Author of 'The Time Machine.' *Second Edition. Crown 8vo.* 6s.

'The ordinary reader of fiction may be glad to know that these stories are eminently readable from one cover to the other, but they are more than that; they are the impressions of a very striking imagination, which, it would seem, has a great deal within its reach.'—*Saturday Review.*

**H. G. Wells.** THE PLATTNER STORY AND OTHERS. By H. G. WELLS. *Second Edition. Crown 8vo.* 6s.

'Weird and mysterious, they seem to hold the reader as by a magic spell.'—*Scotsman.*
'Such is the fascination of this writer's skill that you unhesitatingly prophesy that none of the many readers, however his flesh do creep, will relinquish the volume ere he has read from first word to last.'—*Black and White.*
'No volume has appeared for a long time so likely to give equal pleasure to the simplest reader and to the most fastidious critic.'—*Academy.*
'Mr. Wells is a magician skilled in wielding that most potent of all spells—the fear of the unknown.'—*Daily Telegraph.*

**E. F. Benson.** DODO: A DETAIL OF THE DAY. By E. F. BENSON. *Sixteenth Edition. Crown 8vo.* 6s.

'A delightfully witty sketch of society.'—*Spectator.*
'A perpetual feast of epigram and paradox.'—*Speaker.*

**E. F. Benson.** THE RUBICON. By E. F. BENSON, Author of 'Dodo.' *Fifth Edition. Crown 8vo.* 6s.

'An exceptional achievement; a notable advance on his previous work.'—*National Observer.*

**Mrs. Oliphant.** SIR ROBERT'S FORTUNE. By MRS. OLIPHANT. *Crown 8vo.* 6s.

'Full of her own peculiar charm of style and simple, subtle character-painting comes her new gift, the delightful story before us. The scene mostly lies in the moors, and at the touch of the authoress a Scotch moor becomes a living thing, strong, tender, beautiful, and changeful.'—*Pall Mall Gazette.*

**Mrs. Oliphant.** THE TWO MARYS. By Mrs. Oliphant. *Second Edition. Crown 8vo. 6s.*

**W. E. Norris.** MATTHEW AUSTIN. By W. E. Norris, Author of 'Mademoiselle de Mersac,' etc. *Fourth Edition. Crown 8vo. 6s.*

'"Matthew Austin" may safely be pronounced one of the most intellectually satisfactory and morally bracing novels of the current year.'—*Daily Telegraph.*

**W. E. Norris.** HIS GRACE. By W. E. Norris. *Third Edition. Crown 8vo. 6s.*

'Mr. Norris has drawn a really fine character in the Duke of Hurstbourne, at once unconventional and very true to the conventionalities of life.'—*Athenæum.*

**W. E. Norris.** THE DESPOTIC LADY AND OTHERS. By W. E. Norris. *Crown 8vo. 6s.*

'A budget of good fiction of which no one will tire.'—*Scotsman.*

**W. E. Norris.** CLARISSA FURIOSA. By W. E. Norris, Author of 'The Rogue,' etc. *Crown 8vo. 6s.*

'One of Mr. Norris's very best novels. As a story it is admirable, as a *jeu d'esprit* it is capital, as a lay sermon studded with gems of wit and wisdom it is a model which will not, we imagine, find an efficient imitator.'—*The World.*
'The best novel he has written for some time: a story which is full of admirable character-drawing.'—*The Standard.*

**Robert Barr.** IN THE MIDST OF ALARMS. By Robert Barr. *Third Edition. Crown 8vo. 6s.*

'A book which has abundantly satisfied us by its capital humour.'—*Daily Chronicle.*
'Mr. Barr has achieved a triumph whereof he has every reason to be proud.'—*Pall Mall Gazette.*

**J. Maclaren Cobban.** THE KING OF ANDAMAN : A Saviour of Society. By J. Maclaren Cobban. *Crown 8vo. 6s.*

'An unquestionably interesting book. It would not surprise us if it turns out to be the most interesting novel of the season, for it contains one character, at least, who has in him the root of immortality, and the book itself is ever exhaling the sweet savour of the unexpected. . . . Plot is forgotten and incident fades, and only the really human endures, and throughout this book there stands out in bold and beautiful relief its high-souled and chivalric protagonist, James the Master of Hutcheon, the King of Andaman himself.'—*Pall Mall Gazette.*

**J. Maclaren Cobban.** WILT THOU HAVE THIS WOMAN? By J. M. Cobban, Author of 'The King of Andaman.' *Crown 8vo. 6s.*

'Mr. Cobban has the true story-teller's art. He arrests attention at the outset, and he retains it to the end.'—*Birmingham Post.*

**H. Morrah.** A SERIOUS COMEDY. By Herbert Morrah. *Crown 8vo. 6s.*

'This volume is well worthy of its title. The theme has seldom been presented with more freshness or more force.'—*Scotsman.*

**H. Morrah.** THE FAITHFUL CITY. By HERBERT MORRAH, Author of 'A Serious Comedy.' *Crown 8vo. 6s.*

'Conveys a suggestion of weirdness and horror, until finally he convinces and enthrals the reader with his mysterious savages, his gigantic tower, and his uncompromising men and women. This is a haunting, mysterious book, not without an element of stupendous grandeur.'—*Athenæum.*

**L. B. Walford.** SUCCESSORS TO THE TITLE. By MRS. WALFORD, Author of 'Mr. Smith,' etc. *Second Edition. Crown 8vo. 6s.*

'The story is fresh and healthy from beginning to finish; and our liking for the two simple people who are the successors to the title mounts steadily, and ends almost in respect.'—*Scotsman.*

**T. L. Paton.** A HOME IN INVERESK. By T. L. PATON. *Crown 8vo. 6s.*

'A pleasant and well-written story.'—*Daily Chronicle.*

**John Davidson.** MISS ARMSTRONG'S AND OTHER CIRCUMSTANCES. By JOHN DAVIDSON. *Crown 8vo. 6s.*

'Throughout the volume there is a strong vein of originality, and a knowledge of human nature that are worthy of the highest praise.'—*Scotsman.*

**M. M. Dowie.** GALLIA. By MÉNIE MURIEL DOWIE, Author of 'A Girl in the Carpathians.' *Third Edition. Crown 8vo. 6s.*

'The style is generally admirable, the dialogue not seldom brilliant, the situations surprising in their freshness and originality, while the subsidiary as well as the principal characters live and move, and the story itself is readable from title-page to colophon.'—*Saturday Review.*

**J. A. Barry.** IN THE GREAT DEEP: TALES OF THE SEA. By J. A. BARRY. Author of 'Steve Brown's Bunyip.' *Crown 8vo. 6s.*

'A collection of really admirable short stories of the sea, very simply told, and placed before the reader in pithy and telling English.'—*Westminster Gazette.*

**J. B. Burton.** IN THE DAY OF ADVERSITY. By J. BLOUNDELLE BURTON.' *Second Edition. Crown 8vo. 6s.*

'Unusually interesting and full of highly dramatic situations.'—*Guardian.*

**J. B. Burton.** DENOUNCED. By J. BLOUNDELLE BURTON. *Second Edition. Crown 8vo. 6s.*

The plot is an original one, and the local colouring is laid on with a delicacy and an accuracy of detail which denote the true artist.'—*Broad Arrow.*

**W. C. Scully.** THE WHITE HECATOMB. By W. C. SCULLY, Author of 'Kafir Stories.' *Crown 8vo. 6s.*

'The author is so steeped in Kaffir lore and legend, and so thoroughly well acquainted with native sagas and traditional ceremonial that he is able to attract the reader by the easy familiarity with which he handles his characters.'—*South Africa.*
'It reveals a marvellously intimate understanding of the Kaffir mind, allied with literary gifts of no mean order.'—*African Critic.*

**H. Johnston.** DR. CONGALTON'S LEGACY. By HENRY JOHNSTON. *Crown 8vo. 6s.*

'A worthy and permanent contribution to Scottish literature.'—*Glasgow Herald.*

**J. F. Brewer.** THE SPECULATORS. By J. F. BREWER. *Second Edition. Crown 8vo. 6s.*
'A pretty bit of comedy. . . . It is undeniably a clever book.'—*Academy.*
'A clever and amusing story. It makes capital out of the comic aspects of culture, and will be read with amusement by every intellectual reader.'—*Scotsman.*
'A remarkably clever study.'—*Vanity Fair.*

**Julian Corbett.** A BUSINESS IN GREAT WATERS. By JULIAN CORBETT. *Crown 8vo. 6s.*
'Mr. Corbett writes with immense spirit, and the book is a thoroughly enjoyable one in all respects. The salt of the ocean is in it, and the right heroic ring resounds through its gallant adventures.'—*Speaker.*

**L. Cope Cornford.** CAPTAIN JACOBUS: A ROMANCE OF THE ROAD. By L. COPE CORNFORD. Illustrated. *Crown 8vo. 6s.*
'An exceptionally good story of adventure and character.'—*World.*

**C. P. Wolley.** THE QUEENSBERRY CUP. A Tale of Adventure. By CLIVE PHILLIPS WOLLEY. *Illustrated. Crown 8vo. 6s.*
'A book which will delight boys: a book which upholds the healthy schoolboy code of morality.'—*Scotsman.*

**L. Daintrey.** THE KING OF ALBERIA. A Romance of the Balkans. By LAURA DAINTREY. *Crown 8vo. 6s.*
'Miss Daintrey seems to have an intimate acquaintance with the people and politics of the Balkan countries in which the scene of her lively and picturesque romance is laid.'—*Glasgow Herald.*

**M. A. Owen.** THE DAUGHTER OF ALOUETTE. By MARY A. OWEN. *Crown 8vo. 6s.*
A story of life among the American Indians.
'A fascinating story.'—*Literary World.*

**Mrs. Pinsent.** CHILDREN OF THIS WORLD. By ELLEN F. PINSENT, Author of 'Jenny's Case.' *Crown 8vo. 6s.*
'Mrs. Pinsent's new novel has plenty of vigour, variety, and good writing. There are certainty of purpose, strength of touch, and clearness of vision.'—*Athenæum.*

**Clark Russell.** MY DANISH SWEETHEART. By W. CLARK RUSSELL, Author of 'The Wreck of the Grosvenor,' etc. *Illustrated. Fourth Edition. Crown 8vo. 6s.*

**G. Manville Fenn.** AN ELECTRIC SPARK. By G. MANVILLE FENN, Author of 'The Vicar's Wife,' 'A Double Knot,' etc. *Second Edition. Crown 8vo. 6s.*

**L. S. McChesney.** UNDER SHADOW OF THE MISSION. By L. S. MCCHESNEY. *Crown 8vo. 6s.*
'Those whose minds are open to the finer issues of life, who can appreciate graceful thought and refined expression of it, from them this volume will receive a welcome as enthusiastic as it will be based on critical knowledge.'—*Church Times.*

**Ronald Ross.** THE SPIRIT OF STORM. By RONALD ROSS, Author of 'The Child of Ocean.' *Crown 8vo. 6s.*
A romance of the Sea. 'Weird, powerful, and impressive.'—*Black and White.*

## Messrs. Methuen's List

**R. Pryce.** TIME AND THE WOMAN. By RICHARD PRYCE. *Second Edition. Crown 8vo. 6s.*

**Mrs. Watson.** THIS MAN'S DOMINION. By the Author of 'A High Little World.' *Second Edition. Crown 8vo. 6s.*

**Marriott Watson.** DIOGENES OF LONDON. By H. B. MARRIOTT WATSON. *Crown 8vo. Buckram. 6s.*

**M. Gilchrist.** THE STONE DRAGON. By MURRAY GILCHRIST. *Crown 8vo. Buckram. 6s.*

'The author's faults are atoned for by certain positive and admirable merits. The romances have not their counterpart in modern literature, and to read them is a unique experience.'—*National Observer.*

**E. Dickinson.** A VICAR'S WIFE. By EVELYN DICKINSON. *Crown 8vo. 6s.*

**E. M. Gray.** ELSA. By E. M'QUEEN GRAY. *Crown 8vo. 6s.*

### THREE-AND-SIXPENNY NOVELS 3/6
*Crown 8vo.*

DERRICK VAUGHAN, NOVELIST. By EDNA LYALL.
MARGERY OF QUETHER. By S. BARING GOULD.
JACQUETTA. By S. BARING GOULD.
SUBJECT TO VANITY. By MARGARET BENSON.
THE SIGN OF THE SPIDER. By BERTRAM MITFORD.
THE MOVING FINGER. By MARY GAUNT.
JACO TRELOAR. By J. H. PEARCE.
THE DANCE OF THE HOURS. By 'VERA.'
A WOMAN OF FORTY. By ESMÉ STUART.
A CUMBERER OF THE GROUND. By CONSTANCE SMITH.
THE SIN OF ANGELS. By EVELYN DICKINSON.
AUT DIABOLUS AUT NIHIL. By X. L.
THE COMING OF CUCULAIN. By STANDISH O'GRADY.
THE GODS GIVE MY DONKEY WINGS. By ANGUS EVAN ABBOTT.
THE STAR GAZERS. By G. MANVILLE FENN.
THE POISON OF ASPS. By R. ORTON PROWSE.
THE QUIET MRS. FLEMING. By R. PRYCE.
DISENCHANTMENT. By F. MABEL ROBINSON.
THE SQUIRE OF WANDALES. By A. SHIELD.
A REVEREND GENTLEMAN. By J. M. COBBAN.

A DEPLORABLE AFFAIR. By W. E. NORRIS.
A CAVALIER'S LADYE. By Mrs. DICKER.
THE PRODIGALS. By Mrs. OLIPHANT.
THE SUPPLANTER. By P. NEUMANN.
A MAN WITH BLACK EYELASHES. By H. A. KENNEDY.
A HANDFUL OF EXOTICS. By S. GORDON.
AN ODD EXPERIMENT. By HANNAH LYNCH.

### HALF-CROWN NOVELS    2/6
*A Series of Novels by popular Authors.*

1. HOVENDEN, V.C. By F. MABEL ROBINSON.
2. ELI'S CHILDREN. By G. MANVILLE FENN.
3. A DOUBLE KNOT. By G. MANVILLE FENN.
4. DISARMED. By M. BETHAM EDWARDS.
5. A MARRIAGE AT SEA. By W. CLARK RUSSELL.
6. IN TENT AND BUNGALOW. By the Author of 'Indian Idylls.'
7. MY STEWARDSHIP. By E. M'QUEEN GRAY.
8. JACK'S FATHER. By W. E. NORRIS.
9. JIM B.
10. THE PLAN OF CAMPAIGN. By F. MABEL ROBINSON.
11. MR. BUTLER'S WARD. By F. MABEL ROBINSON.
12. A LOST ILLUSION. By LESLIE KEITH.

**Lynn Linton.** THE TRUE HISTORY OF JOSHUA DAVIDSON, Christian and Communist. By E. LYNN LINTON. *Eleventh Edition. Post 8vo.* 1s.

## Books for Boys and Girls    3/6
*A Series of Books by well-known Authors, well illustrated.*

1. THE ICELANDER'S SWORD. By S. BARING GOULD.
2. TWO LITTLE CHILDREN AND CHING. By EDITH E. CUTHELL.
3. TODDLEBEN'S HERO. By M. M. BLAKE.
4. ONLY A GUARD-ROOM DOG. By EDITH E. CUTHELL.
5. THE DOCTOR OF THE JULIET. By HARRY COLLINGWOOD.
6. MASTER ROCKAFELLAR'S VOYAGE. By W. CLARK RUSSELL.
7. SYD BELTON : Or, The Boy who would not go to Sea. By G. MANVILLE FENN.

## The Peacock Library

*A Series of Books for Girls by well-known Authors, handsomely bound in blue and silver, and well illustrated.* **3/6**

1. A PINCH OF EXPERIENCE. By L. B. WALFORD.
2. THE RED GRANGE. By Mrs. MOLESWORTH.
3. THE SECRET OF MADAME DE MONLUC. By the Author of 'Mdle Mori.'
4. DUMPS. By Mrs. PARR, Author of 'Adam and Eve.'
5. OUT OF THE FASHION. By L. T. MEADE.
6. A GIRL OF THE PEOPLE. By L. T. MEADE.
7. HEPSY GIPSY. By L. T. MEADE. 2s. 6d.
8. THE HONOURABLE MISS. By L. T. MEADE.
9. MY LAND OF BEULAH. By Mrs. LEITH ADAMS.

## University Extension Series

A series of books on historical, literary, and scientific subjects, suitable for extension students and home-reading circles. Each volume is complete in itself, and the subjects are treated by competent writers in a broad and philosophic spirit.

Edited by J. E. SYMES, M.A.,
Principal of University College, Nottingham.

*Crown 8vo. Price (with some exceptions) 2s. 6d.*

*The following volumes are ready:*—

THE INDUSTRIAL HISTORY OF ENGLAND. By H. DE B. GIBBINS, D.Litt., M.A., late Scholar of Wadham College, Oxon., Cobden Prizeman. *Fifth Edition, Revised. With Maps and Plans.* 3s.
'A compact and clear story of our industrial development. A study of this concise but luminous book cannot fail to give the reader a clear insight into the principal phenomena of our industrial history. The editor and publishers are to be congratulated on this first volume of their venture, and we shall look with expectant interest for the succeeding volumes of the series.'—*University Extension Journal.*

A HISTORY OF ENGLISH POLITICAL ECONOMY. By L. L. PRICE, M.A., Fellow of Oriel College, Oxon. *Second Edition.*

PROBLEMS OF POVERTY: An Inquiry into the Industrial Conditions of the Poor. By J. A. HOBSON, M.A. *Third Edition.*

VICTORIAN POETS. By A. SHARP.

THE FRENCH REVOLUTION. By J. E. SYMES, M.A.

PSYCHOLOGY. By F. S. GRANGER, M.A.

THE EVOLUTION OF PLANT LIFE: Lower Forms. By G. MASSEE. *With Illustrations.*

AIR AND WATER. Professor V. B. LEWES, M.A. *Illustrated.*

THE CHEMISTRY OF LIFE AND HEALTH. By C. W. KIMMINS, M.A. *Illustrated.*

THE MECHANICS OF DAILY LIFE. By V. P. SELLS, M.A. *Illustrated.*

ENGLISH SOCIAL REFORMERS. H. DE B. GIBBINS, D.Litt., M.A.

ENGLISH TRADE AND FINANCE IN THE SEVENTEENTH CENTURY. By W. A. S. HEWINS, B.A.

THE CHEMISTRY OF FIRE. The Elementary Principles of Chemistry. By M. M. PATTISON MUIR, M.A. *Illustrated.*

A TEXT-BOOK OF AGRICULTURAL BOTANY. By M. C. POTTER, M.A., F.L.S. *Illustrated.* 3s. 6d.

THE VAULT OF HEAVEN. A Popular Introduction to Astronomy. By R. A. GREGORY. *With numerous Illustrations.*

METEOROLOGY. The Elements of Weather and Climate. By H. N. DICKSON, F.R.S.E., F.R. Met. Soc. *Illustrated.*

A MANUAL OF ELECTRICAL SCIENCE. By GEORGE J. BURCH, M.A. *With numerous Illustrations.* 3s.

THE EARTH. An Introduction to Physiography. By EVAN SMALL, M.A. *Illustrated.*

INSECT LIFE. By F. W. THEOBALD, M.A. *Illustrated.*

ENGLISH POETRY FROM BLAKE TO BROWNING. By W. M. DIXON, M.A.

ENGLISH LOCAL GOVERNMENT. By E. JENKS, M.A., Professor of Law at University College, Liverpool.

THE GREEK VIEW OF LIFE. By G. L. DICKINSON, Fellow of King's College, Cambridge. *Second Edition.*

# Social Questions of To-day

### Edited by H. DE B. GIBBINS, D.Litt., M.A.
### *Crown 8vo.* 2s. 6d.

**2/6**

A series of volumes upon those topics of social, economic, and industrial interest that are at the present moment foremost in the public mind. Each volume of the series is written by an author who is an acknowledged authority upon the subject with which he deals.

*The following Volumes of the Series are ready:—*

TRADE UNIONISM—NEW AND OLD. By G. HOWELL, Author of 'The Conflicts of Capital and Labour.' *Second Edition.*

THE CO-OPERATIVE MOVEMENT TO-DAY. By G. J. HOLYOAKE, Author of 'The History of Co-Operation.' *Second Edition.*

MUTUAL THRIFT. By Rev. J. FROME WILKINSON, M.A., Author of 'The Friendly Society Movement.'

PROBLEMS OF POVERTY: An Inquiry into the Industrial Conditions of the Poor. By J. A. HOBSON, M.A. *Third Edition.*

THE COMMERCE OF NATIONS. By C. F. BASTAPLE, M.A., Professor of Economics at Trinity College, Dublin.

THE ALIEN INVASION. By W. H. WILKINS, B.A., Secretary to the Society for Preventing the Immigration of Destitute Aliens.

THE RURAL EXODUS. By P. ANDERSON GRAHAM.

LAND NATIONALIZATION. By HAROLD COX, B.A.

A SHORTER WORKING DAY. By H. DE B. GIBBINS, D.Litt., M.A., and R. A. HADFIELD, of the Hecla Works, Sheffield.

BACK TO THE LAND: An Inquiry into the Cure for Rural Depopulation. By H. E. MOORE.

TRUSTS, POOLS AND CORNERS: As affecting Commerce and Industry. By J. STEPHEN JEANS, M.R.I., F.S.S.

THE FACTORY SYSTEM. By R. COOKE TAYLOR.

THE STATE AND ITS CHILDREN. By GERTRUDE TUCKWELL.

WOMEN'S WORK. By LADY DILKE, Miss BULLEY, and Miss WHITLEY.

MUNICIPALITIES AT WORK. The Municipal Policy of Six Great Towns, and its Influence on their Social Welfare. By FREDERICK DOLMAN.

SOCIALISM AND MODERN THOUGHT. By M. KAUFMANN.

THE HOUSING OF THE WORKING CLASSES. By R. F. BOWMAKER.

MODERN CIVILIZATION IN SOME OF ITS ECONOMIC ASPECTS. By W. CUNNINGHAM, D.D., Fellow of Trinity College, Cambridge.

THE PROBLEM OF THE UNEMPLOYED. By J. A. HOBSON, B.A., Author of 'The Problems of Poverty.'

LIFE IN WEST LONDON. By ARTHUR SHERWELL, M.A. *Second Edition.*

## Classical Translations

Edited by H. F. FOX, M.A., Fellow and Tutor of Brasenose College, Oxford.

Messrs. Methuen are issuing a New Series of Translations from the Greek and Latin Classics. They have enlisted the services of some of the best Oxford and Cambridge Scholars, and it is their intention that the Series shall be distinguished by literary excellence as well as by scholarly accuracy.

ÆSCHYLUS—Agamemnon, Chöephoroe, Eumenides. Translated by LEWIS CAMPBELL, LL.D., late Professor of Greek at St. Andrews, 5s.

CICERO—De Oratore I. Translated by E. N. P. MOOR, M.A. 3s. 6d.

CICERO — Select Orations (Pro Milone, Pro Murena, Philippic II., In Catilinam). Translated by H. E. D. BLAKISTON, M.A., Fellow and Tutor of Trinity College, Oxford. 5s.

CICERO—De Natura Deorum. Translated by F. BROOKS, M.A., late Scholar of Balliol College, Oxford. 3s. 6d.

LUCIAN—Six Dialogues (Nigrinus, Icaro-Menippus, The Cock, The Ship, The Parasite, The Lover of Falsehood). Translated by S. T. IRWIN, M.A., Assistant Master at Clifton ; late Scholar of Exeter College, Oxford. 3s. 6d.

SOPHOCLES—Electra and Ajax. Translated by E. D. A. MORSHEAD, M.A., Assistant Master at Winchester. 2s. 6d.

TACITUS—Agricola and Germania. Translated by R. B. TOWNSHEND, late Scholar of Trinity College, Cambridge. 2s. 6d.

# Educational Books

## CLASSICAL

PLAUTI BACCHIDES. Edited with Introduction, Commentary, and Critical Notes by J. M'COSH, M.A. *Fcap. 4to.* 12s. 6d.

'The notes are copious, and contain a great deal of information that is good and useful.'—*Classical Review.*

TACITI AGRICOLI With Introduction, Notes, Map, etc. By R. F. DAVIS, M.A., Assistant Master at Weymouth College. *Crown 8vo.* 2s.

TACITI GERMANIA. By the same Editor. *Crown 8vo.* 2s.

HERODOTUS: EASY SELECTIONS. With Vocabulary. By A. C. LIDDELL, M.A., Assistant Master at Nottingham High School. *Fcap. 8vo.* 1s. 6d.

SELECTIONS FROM THE ODYSSEY. By E. D. STONE, M.A., late Assistant Master at Eton. *Fcap. 8vo.* 1s. 6d.

PLAUTUS: THE CAPTIVI. Adapted for Lower Forms by J. H. FRESSE, M.A., late Fellow of St. John's, Cambridge. 1s. 6d.

DEMOSTHENES AGAINST CONON AND CALLICLES. Edited with Notes and Vocabulary, by F. DARWIN SWIFT, M.A., formerly Scholar of Queen's College, Oxford; Assistant Master at Denstone College. *Fcap. 8vo.* 2s.

## GERMAN

A COMPANION GERMAN GRAMMAR. By H. DE B. GIBBINS, D.Litt., M.A., Assistant Master at Nottingham High School. *Crown 8vo.* 1s. 6d.

GERMAN PASSAGES FOR UNSEEN TRANSLATION. By E. M'QUEEN GRAY. *Crown 8vo.* 2s. 6d.

## SCIENCE

THE WORLD OF SCIENCE. Including Chemistry, Heat, Light, Sound, Magnetism, Electricity, Botany, Zoology, Physiology, Astronomy, and Geology. By R. ELLIOTT STEEL, M.A., F.C.S. 147 Illustrations. *Second Edition. Crown 8vo.* 2s. 6d.

'If Mr. Steel is to be placed second to any for this quality of lucidity, it is only to Huxley himself; and to be named in the same breath with this master of the craft of teaching is to be accredited with the clearness of style and simplicity of arrangement that belong to thorough mastery of a subject.'—*Parents' Review.*

ELEMENTARY LIGHT. By R. E. STEEL. With numerous Illustrations. *Crown 8vo.* 4s. 6d.

## MESSRS. METHUEN'S LIST

### ENGLISH

ENGLISH RECORDS. A Companion to the History of England. By H. E. MALDEN, M.A. *Crown 8vo.* 3*s.* 6*d.*

A book which aims at concentrating information upon dates, genealogy, officials, constitutional documents, etc., which is usually found scattered in different volumes.

THE ENGLISH CITIZEN: HIS RIGHTS AND DUTIES. By H. E. MALDEN, M.A. 1*s.* 6*d.*

'The book goes over the same ground as is traversed in the school books on this subject written to satisfy the requirements of the Education Code. It would serve admirably the purposes of a text-book, as it is well based in historical facts, and keeps quite clear of party matters.'—*Scotsman.*

### METHUEN'S COMMERCIAL SERIES
Edited by H. DE B. GIBBINS, D.Litt., M.A.

BRITISH COMMERCE AND COLONIES FROM ELIZABETH TO VICTORIA. By H. DE B. GIBBINS, D.Litt., M.A., Author of 'The Industrial History of England,' etc., etc., 2*s.*

COMMERCIAL EXAMINATION PAPERS. By H. DE B. GIBBINS, D.Litt., M.A., 1*s.* 6*d.*

THE ECONOMICS OF COMMERCE. By H. DE B. GIBBINS, D.Litt., M.A. 1*s.* 6*d.*

A MANUAL OF FRENCH COMMERCIAL CORRESPONDENCE. By S. E. BALLY, Modern Language Master at the Manchester Grammar School. 2*s.*

GERMAN COMMERCIAL CORRESPONDENCE. By S. E. BALLY, Assistant Master at the Manchester Grammar School. *Crown 8vo.* 2*s.* 6*d.*

A FRENCH COMMERCIAL READER. By S. E. BALLY. 2*s.*

COMMERCIAL GEOGRAPHY, with special reference to Trade Routes, New Markets, and Manufacturing Districts. By L. W. LYDE, M.A., of the Academy, Glasgow. 2*s.*

A PRIMER OF BUSINESS. By S. JACKSON, M.A. 1*s.* 6*d.*

COMMERCIAL ARITHMETIC. By F. G. TAYLOR, M.A. 1*s.* 6*d.*

PRÉCIS WRITING AND OFFICE CORRESPONDENCE. By E. E. WHITFIELD, M.A.

### WORKS BY A. M. M. STEDMAN, M.A.

INITIA LATINA: Easy Lessons on Elementary Accidence. *Second Edition. Fcap. 8vo.* 1*s.*

FIRST LATIN LESSONS. *Fourth Edition. Crown 8vo.* 2*s.*

FIRST LATIN READER. With Notes adapted to the Shorter Latin Primer and Vocabulary. *Third Edition.* 18*mo.* 1*s.* 6*d.*

EASY SELECTIONS FROM CAESAR. Part I. The Helvetian War. 18*mo.* 1*s.*

EASY SELECTIONS FROM LIVY. Part I. The Kings of Rome. 18*mo.* 1*s.* 6*d.*

EASY LATIN PASSAGES FOR UNSEEN TRANSLATION. *Fifth Edition. Fcap. 8vo.* 1*s.* 6*d.*

EXEMPLA LATINA. First Lessons in Latin Accidence. With Vocabulary. *Crown 8vo.* 1*s.*

EASY LATIN EXERCISES ON THE SYNTAX OF THE SHORTER AND REVISED LATIN PRIMER. With Vocabulary. *Sixth Edition. Crown 8vo.* 2*s.* 6*d.* Issued with the consent of Dr. Kennedy.

THE LATIN COMPOUND SENTENCE: Rules and Exercises. *Crown 8vo.* 1*s.* 6*d.* With Vocabulary. 2*s.*
NOTANDA QUAEDAM: Miscellaneous Latin Exercises on Common Rules and Idioms. *Third Edition. Fcap. 8vo.* 1*s.* 6*d.* With Vocabulary. 2*s.*
LATIN VOCABULARIES FOR REPETITION: Arranged according to Subjects. *Sixth Edition. Fcap. 8vo.* 1*s.* 6*d.*
A VOCABULARY OF LATIN IDIOMS AND PHRASES. 18*mo.* 1*s.*
STEPS TO GREEK. 18*mo.* 1*s.*
EASY GREEK PASSAGES FOR UNSEEN TRANSLATION. *Second Edition. Fcap. 8vo.* 1*s.* 6*d.*
GREEK VOCABULARIES FOR REPETITION. Arranged according to Subjects. *Second Edition. Fcap. 8vo.* 1*s.* 6*d.*
GREEK TESTAMENT SELECTIONS. For the use of Schools. *Third Edition.* With Introduction, Notes, and Vocabulary. *Fcap. 8vo.* 2*s.* 6*d.*
STEPS TO FRENCH. *Second Edition.* 18*mo.* 8*d.*
FIRST FRENCH LESSONS. *Second Edition. Crown 8vo.* 1*s.*
EASY FRENCH PASSAGES FOR UNSEEN TRANSLATION. *Second Edition. Fcap. 8vo.* 1*s.* 6*d.*
EASY FRENCH EXERCISES ON ELEMENTARY SYNTAX. With Vocabulary. *Crown 8vo.* 2*s.* 6*d.*
FRENCH VOCABULARIES FOR REPETITION: Arranged according to Subjects. *Fifth Edition. Fcap. 8vo.* 1*s.*

## SCHOOL EXAMINATION SERIES
EDITED BY A. M. M. STEDMAN, M.A. *Crown 8vo.* 2*s.* 6*d.*
FRENCH EXAMINATION PAPERS IN MISCELLANEOUS GRAMMAR AND IDIOMS. By A. M. M. STEDMAN, M.A. *Ninth Edition.*
A KEY, issued to Tutors and Private Students only, to be had on application to the Publishers. *Fourth Edition. Crown 8vo.* 6*s. net.*
LATIN EXAMINATION PAPERS IN MISCELLANEOUS GRAMMAR AND IDIOMS. By A. M. M. STEDMAN, M.A. *Seventh Edition.* KEY issued as above. 6*s. net.*
GREEK EXAMINATION PAPERS IN MISCELLANEOUS GRAMMAR AND IDIOMS. By A. M. M. STEDMAN, M.A. *Fifth Edition.* KEY issued as above. 6*s. net.*
GERMAN EXAMINATION PAPERS IN MISCELLANEOUS GRAMMAR AND IDIOMS. By R. J. MORICH, Manchester. *Fifth Edition.* KEY issued as above. 6*s. net.*
HISTORY AND GEOGRAPHY EXAMINATION PAPERS. By C. H. SPENCE, M.A., Clifton College.
SCIENCE EXAMINATION PAPERS. By R. E. STEEL, M.A., F.C.S., Chief Natural Science Master, Bradford Grammar School. *In two vols.* Part I. Chemistry; Part II. Physics.
GENERAL KNOWLEDGE EXAMINATION PAPERS. By A. M. M. STEDMAN, M.A. *Third Edition.* KEY issued as above. 7*s. net.*

Printed by T. and A. CONSTABLE, Printers to Her Majesty
at the Edinburgh University Press

www.ingramcontent.com/pod-product-compliance
Lightning Source LLC
Chambersburg PA
CBHW031337230426
43670CB00006B/357